D1450349

The Bulldog

Our Best Friends

The Beagle

The Boxer

The Bulldog

Caring for Your Mutt

The Dachshund

Ferrets

Fetch this Book

Gerbils

The German Shepherd

The Golden Retriever

Guinea Pigs

Hamsters

The Labrador Retriever

Lizards

The Miniature Schnauzer

Mixed Breed Cats

The Poodle

The Pug

Rabbits

The Rottweiler

The Shih Tzu

Snakes

Turtles

The Yorkshire Terrier

OUR BEST FRIENDS

The Bulldog

Elaine Waldorf Gewirtz

ELDORADO INK

Produced by OTTN Publishing, Stockton, New Jersey

Eldorado Ink
PO Box 100097
Pittsburgh, PA 15233
www.eldoradoink.com

CPSIA compliance information: Batch#101909-2. For further information, contact
Eldorado Ink at info@eldoradoink.com.

First printing

1 3 5 7 9 8 6 4 2

Library of Congress Cataloging-in-Publication Data

   Gewirtz, Elaine Waldorf.
    The bulldog / Elaine Waldorf Gewirtz.
      p. cm. — (Our best friends)
    Includes bibliographical references and index.
    ISBN 978-1-932904-58-1
    1. Bulldog. I. Title.
    SF429.B85G49 2010
    636.72—dc22

                     2009041439

**For information about custom editions, special sales, or premiums,
please contact our special sales department at info@eldoradoink.com.**

TABLE OF CONTENTS

Introduction

GARY KORSGAARD, DVM

The mutually beneficial relationship between humans and animals began long before the dawn of recorded history. Archaeologists believe that humans began to capture and tame wild goats, sheep, and pigs more than 9,000 years ago. These animals were then bred for specific purposes, such as providing humans with a reliable source of food or providing furs and hides that could be used for clothing or the construction of dwellings.

Other animals had been sought for companionship and assistance even earlier. The dog, believed to be the first animal domesticated, began living and working with Stone Age humans in Europe more than 14,000 years ago. Some archaeologists believe that wild dogs and humans were drawn together because both hunted the same prey. By taming and training dogs, humans became more effective hunters. Dogs, meanwhile, enjoyed the social contact with humans and benefited from greater access to food and warm shelter. Dogs soon became beloved pets as well as trusted workers. This can be seen from the many artifacts depicting dogs that have been found at ancient sites in Asia, Europe, North America, and the Middle East.

The earliest domestic cats appeared in the Middle East about 5,000 years ago. Small wild cats were probably first attracted to human settlements because plenty of rodents could be found wherever harvested grain was stored. Cats played a useful role in hunting and killing these pests, and it is likely that grateful humans rewarded them for this assistance. Over time, these small cats gave up some of their aggressive wild behaviors and began living among humans. Cats eventually became so popular in ancient Egypt that they were believed to possess magical powers. Cat statues were placed outside homes to ward off evil spirits, and mummified cats were included in royal tombs to accompany their owners into the afterlife.

Today, few people believe that cats have supernatural powers, but most pet owners feel a magical bond with their pets, whether they are dogs, cats, hamsters, rabbits, horses, or parrots. The lives of pets and their people become inextricably intertwined, providing strong emotional and physical rewards for both humans and animals. People of all ages can benefit from the loving companionship of a pet. Not surprisingly, then, pet ownership is widespread. Recent statistics indicate that about 60 percent of all households in the United States and Canada have at least one pet, while the figure is close to 50 percent of households in the United Kingdom. For millions of people, therefore, pets truly have become their "best friends."

Finding the best animal friend can be a challenge, however. Not only are there many types of domesticated pets, but each has specific needs, characteristics, and personality traits. Even within a category of pets, such as dogs, different breeds will flourish in different surroundings and with different treatment. For example, a German Shepherd may not be the right pet for a person living in a cramped urban apartment; that person might be better off caring for a smaller dog like a Toy Poodle or Shih Tzu, or perhaps a cat. On the other hand, an active person who loves the outdoors may prefer the companion-

ship of a Labrador Retriever to that of a small dog or a passive indoor pet like a goldfish or hamster.

The joys of pet ownership come with certain responsibilities. Bringing a pet into your home and your neighborhood obligates you to care for and train the pet properly. For example, a dog must be housebroken, taught to obey your commands, and trained to behave appropriately when he encounters other people or animals. Owners must also be mindful of their pet's particular nutritional and medical needs.

The purpose of the OUR BEST FRIENDS series is to provide a helpful and comprehensive introduction to pet ownership. Each book contains the basic information a prospective pet owner needs in order to choose the right pet for his or her situation and to care for that pet throughout the pet's lifetime. Training, socialization, proper nutrition, potential medical issues, and the legal responsibilities of pet ownership are thoroughly explained and discussed, and an abundance of expert tips and suggestions are offered. Whether it is a hamster, corn snake, guinea pig, or Labrador Retriever, the books in the OUR BEST FRIENDS series provide everything the reader needs to know about how to have a happy, well-adjusted, and well-behaved pet.

> Despite their "tough" reputation, Bulldogs make great family pets. They are gentle dogs and tend to form strong bonds with children. Bulldogs are also dignified, courageous, and resolute.

CHAPTER ONE

Is a Bulldog Right for You?

With squatty legs, a stout frame, and a large head, flat nose, and big jowls, the Bulldog seems to exude scrappiness. Beneath this plucky exterior, however, is a dog with an amiable and steady disposition. The Bulldog—sometimes called the English Bulldog to distinguish the breed from its smaller French cousin and its larger and more athletic American cousin—is endlessly patient with, and completely devoted to, human companions. A medium-sized, short-haired breed, the Bulldog sports a coat that never requires professional grooming. Nor does the breed require much room or much exercise: A Bulldog would rather stretch out on the sofa with you than chase squirrels around the neighborhood. Plus, with their easy-going nature, Bulldogs don't bark much. For many dog lovers, all of this adds up to an irresistible canine companion. In fact, the Bulldog ranks as the American Kennel Club's eighth most registered breed.

But if you're tempted to jump on the bandwagon and add a Bulldog to your household, there are a few things you should know. Despite its many virtues, this special breed is not exactly low maintenance. Their copious wrinkles and mouthful of odd-shaped teeth must be cleaned every day. Bulldogs slobber a lot. They snore. They don't handle hot weather well and are prone to heatstroke at temperatures as low as 80° Fahrenheit (27° Celsius). When bored or lonely they may chew on just about anything in the house, from furniture to drywall. Bulldogs have a mind of their own, which is a good thing, but sometimes their determination approaches tenacity. If you've never owned a dog before and expect instant obedience with occasional companionship, a Bulldog is probably not a good choice.

THE IDEAL BULLDOG

If you've succumbed to the Bulldog's charms and are considering making a long-term commitment, you might want to investigate the breed standard before choosing your special friend. A breed standard is essentially a written description of the perfect representative of a given purebred dog breed. It is developed by fanciers of the breed, often members of the breed's national parent club.

English Bulldogs have agreeable temperaments, but tend to be protective of their owners.

For Bulldogs in the United States, the national parent club is the Bulldog Club of America.

No dog ever completely achieves the ideal of perfection outlined in a breed standard, which covers physical as well as temperamental characteristics, and even how the dog should move. But breed fanciers and reputable breeders strive to produce dogs that conform as closely as possible to the standard. These dogs can become champions in the show ring.

THE HIGH COST OF BULLDOG PUPS

If you're thinking of buying a Bulldog from a conscientious breeder, be prepared for sticker shock: a good puppy can cost $2,500 to $3,000 or more. Breeders must be making a bundle, right? Wrong. Many breeders consider themselves lucky if they simply break even.

The expenses associated with breeding Bulldogs—when the breeding is done with the goal of producing fine-quality, healthy animals—are considerable. Breeders purchase their first dog from another reputable breeder and pay veterinary expenses. They supply quality dog food, bedding, toys, collars and leashes, microchip identification, and registration and license fees. They may spend several thousand dollars to earn a championship, which confirms the dog's value.

Before breeding a litter, a conscientious breeder will have expensive genetic testing done on the male and the female dog, to ensure that they don't carry any hereditary diseases that might be passed to offspring. After the health clearances have been obtained, the breeder may have to pay a veterinary fertility specialist, as Bulldogs often cannot breed naturally without assistance. Frequently, artificial insemination is required. Puppies must be delivered by caesarean section, and litters are small (usually one to four pups).

After the litter has been whelped, the breeder must monitor mother and puppies constantly. A new Bulldog mother may accidentally roll over on or step on a puppy, which can kill the pup. The breeder must hand-feed the pups or give them to the mother to nurse every two hours.

Growing pups need solid food, immunizations, veterinary checkups, and supplies. Some require emergency veterinary procedures. Breeders pay AKC registrations and local license fees too. When you pick up your puppy, the breeder will hand you a booklet of breed information, puppy care instructions, some food for the first day, and the pedigree.

Add all of this up and the fee you pay for your Bulldog seems like a drop in the bucket.

Breed standards vary slightly, according to the purebred-dog registry in question. In the United States, major registries include the American Kennel Club (AKC) and the United Kennel Club (UKC). England's principal registry is known simply as the Kennel Club, and Canada's is the Canadian Kennel Club. What follows is drawn from the AKC standard.

"The perfect Bulldog," according to the AKC, "must be of medium size and smooth coat; with heavy, thick-set, low-swung body, massive short-faced head, wide shoulders and sturdy limbs. The general appearance and attitude should suggest great stability, vigor and strength."

The AKC breed standard for Bulldogs includes more than two dozen specific attributes, grouped in three categories: "General Properties," "Head," and "Body, Legs, etc." Each attribute is assigned a point value, with the total adding up to 100 points. So, for example, in the "General Properties" category, there are seven attributes, for a total of 22 points: proportion and symmetry (5 points), attitude (3), expression (2), gait (3), size (3), coat

You can find the complete Bulldog breed standard on the AKC's Web site at www.akc.org/breeds/bulldog. The breed standard adopted by the Kennel Club of the United Kingdom can be found online at www.thekennelclub.org.uk/item/155.

(2), and color of coat (4). Regarding size, adult females should weigh in at about 40 pounds (18 kilograms), while males should tip the scales at approximately 50 pounds (22.7 kg). Bulldogs should stand 12 to 14 inches (30.5 to 35.5 centimeters) high at the shoulder. Regarding color of coat, acceptable variations are, in descending order of preference: red brindle; all other brindles; solid white; solid red, fawn, or fallow; and piebald (spotted or patched).

The Bulldog's massive short-faced head is its most prominent physical characteristic, and the AKC breed standard assigns it 39 total points.

FAST FACT

During the 19th century, when British breeders bred out the Bulldog's aggression, they also produced a dog that was shorter, squatter, and less athletic. There were, however, a few dogs with the breed's original appearance in the United States, where earlier British immigrants had brought their Bulldogs. A breeding program that began in the middle of the 20th century sought to preserve this taller, leaner kind of Bulldog. Today, the United Kennel Club recognizes the American Bulldog as a distinct breed. The American Kennel Club, however, does not.

FAST FACT

Tillman, a popular red-and-white Bulldog in Oxnard, California, learned how to skateboard when he was a year old. His talents led to performances on a float in the Rose Parade, on a reality TV show, and at numerous personal appearances.

There are 10 attributes within the category. The skull (5 points) should be very large—at the front of the ears its circumference should at least equal the height of the dog at the shoulders. The jaws (5 points) should be very large, broad, and square, and the dog should have an "underbite." The nose (6 points) should be big, broad, and black. A Bulldog with a brown or liver-colored nose would be disqualified in the show ring.

The "Body, Legs, etc." category includes 12 attributes worth a total of 39 points. Of these, the attributes assigned the most points (5 each) are the shoulders, which should be muscular, very heavy, widespread, and slanting outward; and the back, which should be short and strong, broad at the shoulders and narrow at the loins.

Keep this in mind: A Bulldog that doesn't reach 12 inches at the shoulder, has a less desirable coat

Because of the breed's reputation for toughness and tenacity, many organizations have adopted Bulldogs as mascots. In 1892, Yale became the first university in the United States to adopt an English Bulldog as a mascot. The dog's name was "Handsome Dan"; a large modern-day version of the mascot is pictured on the left. Other groups with Bulldog mascots include the United States Marine Corps (right) and the University of Georgia (inset).

coloration, and sports a brown schnoz won't ever become a champion. But that dog could still make a

FAST FACT

The Bulldog Club in England was founded in 1875, making it the oldest breed club in the world. The Bulldog Club of America, established in 1890, was one of the first breed clubs to join the AKC.

wonderful companion. Before purchasing a Bulldog, ask yourself whether you'll ever want to show or breed your dog. If the answer is an unequivocal no, don't worry so much about conformation to the breed standard.

THE BULLDOG'S PAST

Today's Bulldog has an agreeable, laid-back disposition. But that is only the result of years of selective breeding. During medieval times,

Bulldogs in the British Isles served as working dogs, guarding and driving livestock. By the 13th century, however, people had begun to use these strong and courageous dogs in the cruel activity of bullbaiting. A bull would be tethered with a chain, and a trained Bulldog would be set loose. The dog would attempt to seize the bull by its tender nose, then hold on as the much larger animal thrashed around violently to throw the dog off. Sometimes a dog succeeded in dragging a bull to the ground and pinning it there. But many dogs were gored, trampled, or thrown, suffering serious injuries or even dying in the process. In addition to having powerful jaws, a dog needed to be ferocious, fearless, and nearly impervious to pain to succeed in bullbaiting. Bulldogs were bred for these traits, and the result was a very aggressive breed.

Bullbaiting was a popular spectator sport, but it was also thought to have practical benefits: meat from bulls that had been baited was believed to be more nutritious and tender. In 1835, however, the British Parliament finally outlawed the brutal practice of bullbaiting. Soon the number of Bulldogs in England began to decline dramatically.

Bulldog fanciers stepped in to preserve the breed. They worked to get rid of the Bulldog's aggressiveness and ferocity. Contemporary Bulldog lovers appreciate the fruits of that effort—a breed that, while resolute, has a gentle, affectionate nature.

CHAPTER TWO

Finding the Right Bulldog

After much consideration, you've decided that a wrinkly Bulldog is going to be your new BFF. Your next step is finding the right one for you.

Do you want a puppy or an adult? Do you want a show dog, or are you simply looking for a faithful canine companion? Do you want a male or a female, or is gender unimportant?

Answering these questions will facilitate your search. But whatever your vision of the perfect dog for you, the Bulldog Club of America (BCA) is a helpful resource. On the club's Web site (www.thebca.org) you can find a list of BCA breeders in your area, along with the services they provide. These services may include providing general information, offering puppies

Before making a Bulldog part of your family, think carefully about the characteristics and temperament that you want in a pet.

for sale, offering adult Bulldogs for sale, and rescuing Bulldogs. All BCA breeders have signed the club's code of ethics, which commits them to behaving responsibly toward every Bulldog they breed and following certain guidelines when placing a dog in a new home.

CHOOSING A BREEDER

Depending on where you live, you might have to drive many hours to reach the nearest BCA breeder. If that's not practical, you're not necessarily out of luck. Ask a veterinarian or Bulldog owners for breeder recommendations. You might also

attend a dog show, which is a great place to meet breeders, as well as to learn more about the breed.

It's hard to overstate the importance of finding a reputable breeder if you are getting a puppy, especially if you've never owned a Bulldog before. When you buy a puppy, you're also buying the breeder's expertise. This person should be able to share the latest information about Bulldog behavior, care, health, and training throughout the dog's life.

Comparison-shopping on the basis of price is not a good idea. You might be able to save a few hundred dollars now, but that might cost you

BUYER BEWARE

You're going to have your Bulldog for many years, so spend time to find the ideal breeder and the perfect puppy. Don't buy a puppy just because you see a cute one for sale in a store or at a swap meet. Also don't buy a puppy from an out-of-state breeder and have the dog shipped to you, even if the breeder seems friendly and knowledgeable on the phone, has a professional-looking Web site, and offers photos of your puppy.

Without actually seeing the environment in which your puppy was raised, you have no way of knowing whether the conditions were clean or whether the pup was handled and well socialized. Puppies neglected during their first weeks of life typically grow up to be fearful and shy. They also have difficulty with housetraining. A pet store may offer you a 24- or 48-hour health guarantee, but problems frequently crop up after that period. While a distant breeder may offer a comprehensive health guarantee, you're not likely to ship the dog back if you encounter problems. Always visit the breeder and see the puppies for yourself before agreeing to buy one.

thousands of dollars—and a lot of heartache—later if your new best friend isn't healthy or well adjusted. Find a great breeder you can trust, and a terrific puppy will follow.

Look for a breeder who performs health tests on her stock before breeding to make sure they are free from genetic illnesses, such as heart problems, slipped kneecaps, and hip dysplasia. A good breeder also has a four-generation pedigree for her puppies and can provide details about the appearance, temperament, and health history of all the dogs in that pedigree.

Don't expect to buy a puppy on the day you want one. The best breeders plan litters years in advance and only breed a few each year. Often they have a long waiting list.

In addition, a good breeder will want to know a bit about you before agreeing to sell you a puppy. Expect to be interviewed. The breeder wants to make sure you can provide the right care and training for the

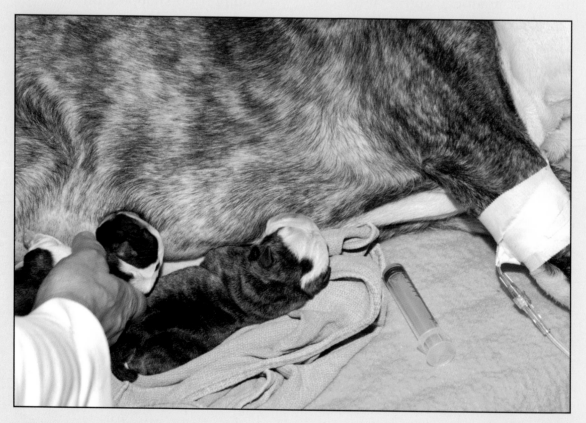

Bulldog puppies begin to nurse as their mother recovers from a cesarean delivery. Nearly all experienced Bulldog breeders have their litters delivered via C-section, because the large size of these dogs' heads makes it difficult for them to fit through the mother's birth canal.

Bulldog she has worked so hard to produce. If she has doubts, she won't sell you a puppy. On the other hand, a great breeder will stand behind her dogs. If you buy a puppy but at some point can no longer care for it, she'll take the dog back.

PICKING A PUPPY

When you visit litters, look for these signs of good health:

- Puppy eyes should be clear, without discharge or redness.
- The puppy should be active and not stay in a corner or remain lying down most of the time.
- The coat should be sleek and shiny, not thin, patchy, dry, or red. There shouldn't be any sores or irritation on the face, feet, or body.
- The puppy should have dry, odor-free ears.
- The puppy should be eager to greet you and want to crawl into your lap.
- The puppy should have a healthy appetite. If possible, try to arrange your visit during feeding time.
- The puppy should not vomit or have diarrhea.
- The puppy should be walking without a limp, and all legs should look straight and strong.

Also, look at the facilities where the pups are being raised. They should be clean, comfortable, and well lit. The pups should have a few interesting toys, a bowl of fresh water, and clean bedding.

If at any time during your visit you feel that something isn't right with the puppy or the sale, follow your instinct and leave without a puppy. You might save yourself thousands of dollars in veterinary expenses and a world of emotional distress.

ADOPTING A BULLDOG

Bulldogs under two years of age are rarely available through rescue groups. When rescue groups do have Bulldog puppies, the puppies may have severe health problems. Breeders, however, sometimes have older puppies or young Bulldogs that didn't work out for the show ring and need homes.

There are pros and cons to adopting an older Bulldog. Usually an adult Bulldog is housetrained, although many rescued adults develop potty-training issues in their new homes. Similarly, while most adult dogs are through with the chewing stage, on occasion an adopted adult Bulldog may regress and start chomping down on the furniture in a new environment. One definite advantage to adopting a mature Bulldog is that medical surprises should be minimal. By the time a Bulldog is two years old, most health problems should already be diagnosed.

If you want to adopt an older dog, contact the Bulldog Club of America's Rescue Network. The club's Web site maintains a list of dogs in need of homes and provides contact information for rescue groups throughout the United States.

THE RIGHT PAPERS

The well-bred Bulldog comes with a pile of papers. Ethical breeders will give you a packet of information when you pick up your puppy. You should receive your dog's pedigree, which is the Bulldog's family tree. The sire's, or father's, line will be on the top half of the paper; the dam's, or mother's, line will be on the bottom. Dogs that have a "Ch" in front of their names were champions. You can be assured that they were outstanding examples of the breed standard. Look over the pedigree, and don't hesitate to ask the breeder any questions that might occur to you. Also ask the breeder to show you photos of the dogs in the pedigree if she has them. It's always interesting to see what your dog's parents and grandparents looked like.

The breeder should also give you the puppy's registration application. Both you and the breeder need to sign it. To register your puppy, the signed form must be mailed to the AKC or the UKC with the correct fee. You'll receive a registration certificate.

Reputable breeders will give you a sales contract. It should state specific health and quality guarantees and refund or replacement policies. Pet-quality puppies are usually sold with AKC limited registration, meaning that they cannot be shown in AKC conformation events and any puppies they may produce will be ineligible for registration with the AKC. You'll also be asked to sign an agreement that you will always care for this puppy throughout her lifetime and never abandon her. If you cannot care for her, the breeder should be notified.

The breeder should provide verification that a veterinarian has examined your puppy, along with the vet's name, address, and phone number. Verification of any immunizations and wormings, along with copies of the parents' or puppies' health tests, should also be included. If there's anything you don't understand, be sure to ask the breeder. You'll also receive a booklet of care instructions and one or two days' worth of food.

Often, Bulldogs are put up for adoption because of a change in the owner's living situation. For example, the owner may be moving into an apartment that doesn't allow pets, or taking a job that won't allow enough time to properly care for her dog. Such dogs typically do not have behavior problems, and can make excellent pets.

According to the Southern California Bulldog Rescue, the average age of Bulldogs available for adoption is five years. While some Bulldogs up for adoption are angels, others come with health or temperament issues, which is the most common reason why Bulldogs are abandoned. Most other dogs are given up when people can no longer afford to care for them.

In an effort to find the best homes for the dogs, Bulldog rescue organizations ask potential new owners to fill out an adoption application. Rescue volunteers are anxious to make sure that new owners understand the breed's craving for attention and clown-like attitude so the

dogs remain in their new homes for the rest of their lives. Besides agreeing to provide an extra dose of love and attention every day, applicants must be willing to accept a few wet kisses and work to solve any social, emotional, or behavioral problems their adopted Bulldog may have. Because there are more people who want to adopt Bulldogs than there are dogs available, you may have to wait a few weeks or months until the right match comes along.

Before you adopt a Bulldog through a rescue organization, the dog should have a veterinary examination and be current on all vaccines. A female should be spayed, and a male neutered. The dog's temperament should be evaluated. Some rescued Bulldogs don't get along with other dogs, and some can't be placed with children, so if you have another dog or if there are children in your home, it may take longer to find an appropriate match.

Know that a rescued Bulldog, while much cheaper than the $1,200 to $2,500 you could expect to pay for a puppy from a reputable breeder, isn't free. You'll be asked to donate between $200 and $700, depending on the health and age of the dog and the individual rescue organization. This donation provides funds for veterinary expenses and the care of Bulldogs in the program.

Once you adopt a Bulldog, expect that it will take some time for your canine companion to adjust to your routine. If for any reason the Bulldog doesn't work out, the rescue organization will accept the dog back.

Bulldogs think water looks like fun and will dive in without an invitation. The problem is that they can't swim and will sink like a rock. For this reason, rescue groups will not grant an adoption if the applicant has a pool that is not securely fenced.

CHAPTER THREE

Bringing Home a Bulldog

You've waited a long time for a Bulldog, and now you're ready to bring your new friend home. Before she enters your life, ask your breeder or rescue coordinator for a list of things your dog will need. Every breed requires different equipment, and Bulldogs are a little picky about their stuff.

Purchase basic supplies before picking up your dog. Your Bulldog's first day at your home will most likely be hectic enough without a last-minute run to the pet store.

If your dog has been eating a packaged commercial dog food, it's best to keep her on the same diet for the first month or so. Once she's

You should purchase a dog bed and other supplies before bringing your new Bulldog home.

accustomed to her new digs, you can change to a different diet if you want.

SHOPPING FOR ESSENTIALS

Besides food, your dog should have a crate. Choose a collapsible wire model, as this type transports easily and permits air to flow around your dog to keep her cool when it's warm. During cold weather you can put a blanket over the top. The crate should be large enough for a full-grown Bulldog to lie down while fully stretched out, and to comfortably stand up and turn around without hitting her head. Don't buy a crate that's too big. Your dog will use the back of it for a restroom, which complicates housetraining.

At night your Bulldog should sleep in her crate, but you may also want to get a padded dog bed she can snooze in during the daytime. These come in all shapes and sizes. Don't buy an expensive one until your dog is out of the chewing stage, which can last up to two years.

Your dog will need a bowl for food and a separate bowl for water. While you'll find a wide assortment of glass, ceramic, plastic, and stainless steel options, choose bowls that can't tip over or slide across the floor. No-tip stainless steel bowls are easy to clean and will last forever. While plastic bowls are the cheapest, puppies love to chew on them. Food particles can get trapped in the resulting cracks. To help keep the

BUDGETING FOR A BULLDOG

Keeping a Bulldog happy and healthy doesn't come cheap. To prepare yourself and your checkbook for the expense of owning a Bulldog, call your veterinarian's office for a rough estimate of these medical costs: worming; spay or neuter surgery; vaccines; annual office visits; dental cleanings; heartworm, tick, and flea preventive medications; and after-hours or emergency treatment. Bulldogs have special needs requiring extra veterinary care.

Walk through your local pet supply store and get price checks for quality commercial dry dog food, treats, collars, leashes, grooming supplies, toys, and a crate. Make sure all this fits into your budget. While you may be able to skimp on a few toys, your dog deserves the best food and medical care you can afford.

water cold, the water dish should be large and deep. The food dish only needs to hold about two cups.

You'll need a leash for your Bulldog. There are many varieties from which to choose. Retractable leashes aren't generally recommended for strong breeds like Bulldogs. In the event of an emergency such as the approach of an aggressive dog, you probably won't be able to reel your Bulldog in quickly enough, and you might cut your hands on the elastic lead. Consider a four- or six-foot leather leash in a width that feels comfortable in your hand. Leather is easy to hold, and it seldom breaks. The Bulldog Club of America recommends putting a lightweight, small-link "choke" collar on your dog when you take her for a walk. Some people prefer harnesses because these don't put pressure on the dog's neck, but harnesses encourage some Bulldogs to pull instead of walking nicely.

Avoid purchasing flimsy toys or cheap balls. A Bulldog will gnaw such items until they fall apart, and the small pieces will pose a choking hazard to your pet.

FAST FACT

Most dogs dislike head halters. This is especially true of Bulldogs, with their unique face shape. A regular collar and leash can be just as effective as a halter.

You'll also need an assortment of grooming supplies (see Chapter 7), and some toys. Avoid small balls and little plush or squeaky toys that your dog can swallow. Select large hard-rubber chew toys, with or without places to tuck away treats. Ropes or long rubber tug toys and Nylabone bones are safe and fun as well.

A Bulldog that gets loose poses a danger to others and is at greater risk of getting injured. Your backyard should have a fence that is sturdy enough to prevent your pet from getting through or under it. Electric fences are usually effective at keeping dogs close to home; however, they may not be deterrent enough to prevent an intact male from chasing a female in heat.

DOG-PROOFING YOUR HOME

Think of your new Bulldog puppy as an uncoordinated, rambunctious toddler. To her your home is a playground filled with interesting things to scratch, sniff, and explore. It's your responsibility to keep your pup safe in this environment.

Every room in your house, in addition to your yard, contains potential hazards to your dog. As a precaution, install baby locks on your cabinets. Put up baby gates to keep your dog out of any rooms that can't be made safe—or rooms that contain valuable items you don't want your dog to ruin.

In rooms where your dog will be allowed to roam, tack loose electrical cords to the wall or enclose them with cable wrap or a cord concealer. This will keep your dog from tripping over or chewing on them. Put all garbage in a bin with a tight-fitting lid, or store the wastebasket in a cabinet. In the bathroom put all hygiene products, used razor blades, medications, and cleaning supplies out of your dog's reach.

In the yard, check fencing and gates for any sharp spots that could hurt your dog. Make sure gates are secure.

The Web site of the American Society for the Prevention of Cruelty

If possible, place kitchen garbage cans inside a cabinet or closet to keep your Bulldog out of the trash.

Electrical cords should be covered or raised so that they are out of your Bulldog's reach.

Azaleas and other common plants can be poisonous to dogs. Check your house and garden carefully before bringing a Bulldog home.

to Animals lists 17 plants that are poisonous to your Bulldog if ingested (www.aspca.org/pet-care/poison-control/plants). Rose bushes pose another hazard. While roses aren't poisonous, they can seriously injure your Bulldog's eyes if she brushes up against the thorns.

COMING HOME

When the time comes to bring your Bulldog home, opt for early in the day. Also, try to pick your dog up at the start of a weekend or while you are on vacation. This will allow you to spend a couple full days or more getting your dog settled into her new home.

In general, the worst time to bring a new dog home is before a major holiday, such as Thanksgiving or Christmas. Often these holidays are accompanied by a lot of excitement and commotion. This is not what your Bulldog needs. After leaving her home—perhaps the only one she's ever known—being thrust into the arms of strangers, and traveling in an odd-smelling vehicle, she's likely to be confused. You should try to provide a quiet, stable environment for a few days to help her adjust to her new surroundings. In fact, many reputable breeders won't send pups home until after the holidays are over.

Your Bulldog puppy should be introduced to each member of his new family. However, never allow dogs and children to play together unsupervised. This rule is to ensure everyone's safety. Most dog bites occur in the home, and children are often the ones bitten. At the same time, a child can easily injure a puppy without intending harm.

When you do bring your new Bulldog home, introduce her to all the members of your household, one person at a time. However, wait a few days before inviting neighbors and extended family over so you don't overwhelm her. Needless to say, this isn't the time to host your child's birthday party or have a family reunion.

Take your new dog on a tour of the house. Don't rush the experience. Give her time to explore each room before moving on to the next. Show your Bulldog where the food and water dishes are kept, but wait a few hours before feeding her. It's normal if she doesn't eat her first meal or two. Bulldogs are adaptable, and yours will probably fit right in soon enough.

THE FIRST NIGHT

Establish a schedule so that your dog will know what to expect. This not only facilitates housetraining but also

PET INSURANCE

With soaring veterinary bills and expensive new treatments available, signing up for pet insurance seems like a good idea. According to the American Pet Products Association, Americans will spend $12.2 billion on veterinary care in 2009.

But while pet insurance coverage can cost $2,000 to $6,000 over the life of an average dog, you might never pay that much for regular treatment. You may come out ahead by putting the same amount into a savings account.

Pet insurance policies have deductibles and co-pays, and they limit how much they will pay out each year. Before buying a policy, read the fine print. Some policies do not cover pre-existing

problems. Also, hereditary conditions likely to affect your Bulldog, such as hip dysplasia, may not be covered.

In the best case the insurance is protection against catastrophic expenses. Shop around, as policies, premiums, deductibles, and co-pays vary among companies.

FAST FACT

Waste disposal systems that can be installed in a yard are available. They use environmentally friendly enzymes and bacteria to turn doggy waste into a ground-absorbed liquid.

helps the dog adapt to your routine. Feed her around the same times, and in the same area. Try to keep to a regular schedule for playtimes and bedtime.

Puppies sleep a lot. Don't be alarmed if your Bulldog suddenly plops down for a snooze in the middle of a game. Make sure she has plenty of rest time during the day—ideally, in her crate. This way she will become accustomed to her special place before it's time to go to bed at night.

A good way to help get your puppy to sleep through the first night in her crate is to put the crate next to your bed. Inside the crate, put a chew toy and a large stuffed animal, but be sure to remove any plastic eyes or pieces she could swallow. The toy will give her something to do if she wakes up during the night, and the plush toy will be a comforting reminder of bunking with her littermates. About an hour before your bedtime, play with your dog to tire her out, and take her outside to use the potty. When she's finished, put her in the crate and turn off the lights in your bedroom.

If she whimpers during the night, you can reassure her that you haven't abandoned her. When dogs are crated alone outside their owners' bedrooms, they're apt to bark and whimper the first few nights. If you think your dog has to use the potty, quickly take her outside. But don't talk to her or give her any extra attention because she'll think it's playtime. Return her to the crate and go back to sleep.

Resist the urge to let your dog sleep in your bed, as this is a bad habit that's very hard to break. She can easily fall off or jump off during the night. This might result in serious injury.

CHAPTER FOUR

Raising a Better Bulldog

Bulldog pups have little regard for doors, and they aren't picky where they leave their streams of saliva. A Bulldog pup may be inclined to gnaw on the chair leg. She thinks nothing of rolling on the good carpet after a romp in the garden.

Good Bulldog manners don't happen by accident. Unless you make some house rules, your new roly-poly puppy won't have a clue which activities are no-no's. Your Bulldog needs to know what you expect, just as she learned her earliest life lessons from her mother, who provided nourishment and comfort, and her littermates, who were a source of warmth and companionship.

Dogs pick up cues from their environment and tailor their behavior

Puppies are extremely cute, but they need careful attention so they don't get into trouble.

FAST FACT

A Bulldog can be trained to do just about anything. If you are a new dog owner, consider sending your dog to a class that uses positive reinforcement, or find a trainer by contacting the Association of Pet Dog Trainers (www.apdt.com).

to achieve their needs. Bulldogs are smart dogs. They watch their owners and are eager to please. Inside that tough exterior is a soft soul waiting to trust you to provide the boundaries.

By using positive training with your dog, you are adding to her natural talents to be a good citizen in your home. As soon as you bring your Bulldog home, start showing her what you expect. This way she won't have time to develop bad habits. Remember that your pup is a natural explorer. Anything you leave in her path is fair game for her teeth. You are responsible for preventing her from getting hold of anything you don't want her to have.

Harsh training methods like shaking or hitting don't work well with a Bulldog—or with any other dog, for that matter. The best way to train a Bulldog is to learn what motivates her, such as a tasty treat, a game of tug, or pats on the head or tummy. When she does something good, reward her immediately so she knows you appreciate what she's done. To express praise, use a pleasant, upbeat tone of voice, and speak a little bit louder than normal. When you're displeased with your dog's behavior, speak in a lower voice.

The first year with a new puppy or dog is fun and exciting. You've selected an intelligent, wonderful breed. So be patient, remain consistent in your training, and enjoy every minute with your Bulldog. It's a special time you'll always remember.

SOCIALIZATION

Your job is to continue your dog's education by providing good socialization. Gradually and in a positive way, socialization introduces your Bulldog to the world around her. The goal of this ongoing process is to create a polite, friendly, outgoing, and confident dog.

Start by slowly introducing your Bulldog to new sights, sounds, and situations. Good socialization doesn't have to be a huge ordeal. In fact, a constant barrage of new experiences will only overwhelm your dog and erode rather than boost her confidence. Taking her outside your home for a few minutes a day to visit one or two new places is plenty.

Wearing her collar with ID tags and a leash, your dog can walk through a pet supply store, go for a walk around the neighborhood or outdoor mall, or ride in the car to visit friends. Meandering through a garden center, going to a park or playground, or observing a construction site that's shut down for the weekend works wonders. These adventures should be short, sweet, and lots of fun.

Go outdoors when the weather is cool. This way your dog won't have to deal with new experiences while feeling uncomfortable at the same time. For your outings, pack a small bag with cleanup bags, a few training treats, wet wipes, a collapsible water bowl and water, and a small towel. The towel comes in handy if you want to take a break and give your dog a cool spot on which to lie down.

When encountering a friendly stranger, simply stop and chat. Your dog will feel your level of relaxation and enjoy the experience. If your Bulldog seems hesitant around someone, ask the person if they wouldn't mind giving your dog a little treat. This creates a positive association with a stranger. Stay away from someone you don't feel comfortable meeting, because your pup will pick

At an early age, your Bulldog must be taught to get along with other friendly dogs.

Opportunities for socialization will occur naturally when you're out for a walk with your Bulldog. Socialization is most important when your dog is eight to twelve weeks old. Ideally, your Bulldog should meet three to five new people or animals each week during this period.

up on your discomfort. Let your pup observe adults and children, but don't let her jump on people.

When you encounter another dog, ask the owner if the dog is gentle.

Only when you feel comfortable with the situation should you let your Bulldog meet a new dog. Watch both of them, and don't let your dog become too exuberant or get too close to the other dog. You can't guarantee another dog's behavior.

CRATE TRAINING

A crate is not a jail. Nor is it cruel and unusual punishment. Think of this small wire or hard-sided kennel as your dog's very own digs, her special place to chill out. A crate is also indispensable when it comes to housetraining your new Bulldog or securing her safely when taking her for a car ride. At the veterinarian's office your dog will be housed in a crate following any surgical procedures, so the sooner you train your dog to feel comfortable in a crate, the better.

Your dog needs time to adjust to her place. Introduce it gradually over several days. For the first session, set up the crate and place a few toys and a blanket inside. Let your dog sniff it out. Encourage her to explore the interior by tossing a treat into the back of the crate. If she wanders in, praise her and quietly close the door for a few seconds. Then praise her again, open the door, and give her another treat when she comes out. Repeat this several times, gradually extending the time your dog is inside the crate to about 10 minutes. Then put her in the crate again, but this time leave the room for one minute before returning to let her out.

Gradually lengthen the time you're gone to 30 minutes.

If your dog simply stands in front of the crate and looks in, encourage her to go after the goodies with some

THE FEARFUL BULLDOG

Once a fierce baiter of bulls, the Bulldog is today a charming and out-going breed that loves people. Still, some Bulldogs are shy and fearful as a result of neglect or improper socialization.

Even stable puppies will go through a fearful stage when they are around four months old. This coincides with teething, and the puppies' mouths hurt. At a year of age, dogs experience a second fearful peri-od that correlates with maturity. This is a time of confusion, caution, and worry. With consistent and proper care, however, you can help your dog through these periods.

To build a shy Bulldog's confidence, never force her to approach a person or an object that worries her. This will only scare her even more. Never yell at or scold her for being frightened, even if she's barking or backing away. Also resist the urge to pick her up when she's shak-ing from fear. This does nothing to build her self-esteem but merely reinforces her fear. Another response that will reinforce your dog's fear is to repeat reassuringly, "It's OK. It's OK."

Instead of these responses, use a nor-mal tone of voice to name and describe the object that is causing your dog's fear. For example, say, "That's an odd looking fire hydrant, isn't it?" To your dog, the words are meaningless, but your calmness reassures her that you're not panicked.

Sometimes giving your dog a treat will help relax her, but if she's so frightened she may just spit it out. That's OK. Move away from the object or situation and offer the treat again. When your dog accepts the food, you'll know she's feeling a little more confident. It may take several trips for your dog to overcome her fear, but eventually she'll figure out that the fire hydrant or tall man who lives down the street won't hurt her.

Make sure that your Bulldog's crate is the proper size. The crate should be large enough for your dog to stand and turn around inside. For adult Bulldogs, a 36-inch (91-cm) crate works best. This may be too large for a puppy, though. Dogs do not like to urinate where they sleep, but if a crate is too large a puppy can make a mess in one corner and sleep comfortably in another. Wire crates like this one often come with dividers, so that the crate's area can be adjusted as your Bulldog grows.

upbeat words. Come dinnertime, put her feeding dish inside the crate to encourage her to go inside. This usually does the trick. When you decide to put your Bulldog in her crate for the evening, place the crate next to your bed. This way you can talk to her and reassure her that you haven't abandoned her. Don't put the crate in another room away from you, as this can be scary to your dog and she'll surely make a fuss.

Keep a can of treats near the crate. Whenever you want her to go inside, shake the container and call your dog at the same time. When she comes to you, throw a treat from the can into the crate. She'll associate the treat with the pleasant experience of going to her bed.

HOUSETRAINING

When it comes to pee and poop, a Bulldog trains quickly. Still, communicating that the hall carpet is not a restroom can be a daunting task for a novice dog owner. It doesn't have to be hard. Forget about using newspapers, puddle pads, or a litter box before having your dog transition to eliminating in the yard. Begin taking her outside as soon as you bring her home. A nine-week-old puppy is not too young to learn where the bathroom is.

For fast housetraining results, use positive training. Reward your dog with kind words and praise when she goes to the bathroom in the right place. Really make a fuss over her so there's no question that you're thrilled with her behavior.

The old method of yelling, hitting, or rubbing a dog's nose in the mess she's made is cruel and doesn't work. Your dog will only go behind your back and pee or poop when you're not looking.

It helps to restrict the area in which you allow your puppy to roam. Choose one or two rooms where you spend most of your time, and close the doors to or place baby gates across all other doorways. This way you can keep an eye out for when your dog needs to go outside without having to search the whole house to find her.

EASY STEPS

You can teach your Bulldog to eliminate outdoors in just six easy steps.

STEP 1: Use a crate. Puppies don't like to pee and poop where they eat and sleep. If you leave the house or can't watch your puppy, put her inside her crate. When you retrieve her from the crate, take her outside to go to the bathroom immediately. Take her outside the minute she wakes up from a nap or first thing in the morning after a good night's sleep.

STEP 2: Designate a potty location. With your dog on a leash, go to the

CANINE BODY LANGUAGE

To facilitate training, read your dog's body language. Signs that indicate fear include a tail pointed downward or tucked under the body, ears drooped or folded back, and eyes wide open showing the whites. When your dog hides behind you or tries to escape, that is another sign of fear.

Happiness is signaled when a tail wags straight out behind or at a slightly elevated position, ears are forward with the head cocked to one side, and eyes are focused but not staring directly at you or another object. A friendly, playful attitude is an obvious sign of happiness.

potty location. Don't walk around. Your dog will sniff the area from the reaches of the leash. When she's exhausted all the new smells, she'll pee or poop. If you walk around, she'll take her time to check out all the new aromas without going to the bathroom.

STEP 3: Stick to a schedule. While awake during the daytime, an adult Bulldog will need to go to the bathroom about every two to three hours. Puppies, whose bladders are a lot smaller, need to go about every 30 minutes when they're not asleep. Also take your dog out after she eats and a few minutes before bedtime. If she has to go to the bathroom in the middle of the night, take her outside but don't play with her. After she does her business, put her back in her crate and turn off the lights.

STEP 4: Watch your dog's body language. Signs that a Bulldog puppy needs to go outside include squatting, turning in circles or pacing back and forth, and sniffing the ground intently. If you see any of these

Housetraining can be frustrating, but with patience and proper training your Bulldog will soon learn that he must always eliminate urine or feces outside.

FAST FACT

Treats facilitate training. To reward your dog for doing what you ask, use bite-size, healthy food treats that your dog doesn't normally receive at home, such as chicken, cheese, hot dogs, or small pieces of apples. Avoid crunchy or chewy treats that take too long to chew and will distract your dog from the lesson.

signs, quickly pick your dog up and carry her outside.

STEP 5: Ignore mistakes. Accidents will happen, even if you stick to a potty schedule and are vigilant about monitoring your dog's body language. When your dog makes a mistake, simply clean it up without complaint. Drawing your dog's attention to the accident will only make the housetraining more difficult.

STEP 6: Be patient. Housetraining requires time. With Bulldogs it takes a few weeks or months before they're reliably housetrained.

BASIC MANNERS

Every Bulldog needs to know a few basic commands. These include "sit," "stay," "down," and "come."

To teach the "sit" command, hold a treat up over your dog's nose and

slowly move it back over her head as you say, "sit." As she moves her head to follow the treat with her eyes, she will naturally drop into a sitting position. When she does, immediately give her the treat and tell her she's a good dog. With a few repetitions, your dog will understand and obey the "sit" command.

Once your dog knows how to sit, teach her the "stay" command. After telling her to sit, say, "stay." Take a few steps backward. If she remains in the stay position for a few seconds, praise her and say, "OK." Then move toward her so she knows she can get up, and give her a treat.

Training a dog to sit is a starting point for teaching other basic obedience commands.

The "down" command can be used to control your Bulldog in public places.

Repeat this several times. Gradually back up a few more steps until you are about 10 feet away from your dog, and gradually extend the time you require your dog to maintain the "stay" position.

To teach the "down" command, start with your dog in a sitting position. Hold a treat in front of her and slowly lower it. This will naturally draw your Bulldog downward until she is stretched out and lying down.

Establish household rules before bringing a dog home, and enforce them consistently. If you don't want your adult Bulldog sitting on your furniture, don't allow him to do this when he's a puppy.

When she reaches that position, immediately give her the treat and praise her. Repeat the exercise until she understands what you want when you say, "down."

The "come" command can be a lifesaver. You may need to use this command if your dog bolts into oncoming traffic or decides to wander off. To teach the command, fill a coffee can with biscuits. While inside the house, shake the can and say your dog's name followed by "come." When she comes to you, lavishly praise her and give her a treat. Once she responds reliably indoors, move to a fenced-in outdoor area to practice the command. Your dog should never be allowed off-leash in an open or public area until she has learned to respond to the "come" command every time.

Taking your dog for a walk should be a pleasure and not a chore. Without training, however, your Bulldog is likely to pull at her leash. To teach her not to pull, simply stop walking when the leash goes taut.

Your Bulldog must be trained to walk without tugging on his leash.

Don't begin walking again until the leash is loose. Eventually your dog will realize that trying to drag you around will get her nowhere.

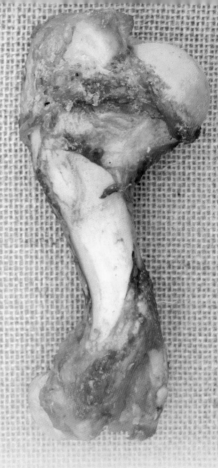

CHAPTER FIVE

Feeding 101

The Bulldog lives to eat. She'll consume anything you feed her. She's also not shy about scrounging up her own snacks from the garden or the garbage.

It's essential that you make sure your dog gets a healthy, balanced diet. Poor food choices that are high in fats and carbohydrates will add inches to your Bulldog's belly and ribs and cause obesity. Other health issues linked to poor-quality diets include skin and ear infections, coat and eye problems, hyperactivity, lethargy, intestinal upset, constipation, arthritis, diabetes, epilepsy, heart disease, and parasites.

While your Bulldog could survive on an inferior diet, enjoying good nutrition enables her to reach her

When it comes to your dog's diet, you'll have important decisions to make. Some Bulldog owners like to feed their pets raw food and bones, while others feel their dogs will thrive on commercially processed foods. Do some research to determine what diet is best for your dog.

full potential and live a better and longer life. Fortunately, you're in charge of what your dog consumes, and you can feed her a healthy diet, whether the basis of that diet is raw, home-cooked, or high-quality commercial dog food.

Like people, dogs are omnivores. While they love meat, dogs need six basic components for good health: water, proteins, carbohydrates, fats, vitamins, and minerals. Proteins are used for growth and repair of muscles, bones, and other body tissues. Carbohydrates metabolize into glucose for energy. Fats are also used for energy, while vitamins and minerals are responsible for muscle and nerve function, bone growth, healing, metabolism, and fluid balance.

WHAT'S IN A LABEL?

It's important to know what your dog is eating. The best way to do that is to read the Association of American Feed Control

Officials (AAFCO) label printed on the dog food package or can. The organization provides an analysis of the ingredients, calories, and nutritional adequacy of the food.

While this does not guarantee the quality of the food, it means that the food is properly labeled, nutritionally balanced, and complete according to AAFCO guidelines. The analysis lists the minimum percentages of protein and fat and the maximum percentages of fiber and water.

The AAFCO requires dry adult food to contain a minimum of 18 percent protein and 5 percent fat. Puppy food must have at least 22 percent protein and 8 percent fat.

Look at the list of ingredients. The order in which the ingredients are listed reflects their proportions in the food, from highest percentage

Stainless steel food and water dishes have several advantages. They are difficult for a dog to knock over, resist damage from chewing, and are easier to keep clean and bacteria-free than plastic bowls.

to lowest. The first ingredient listed should be an animal protein, such as beef or chicken. Another protein source should be listed second or third. The ingredients list should also contain a carbohydrate, fat, vitamins and minerals, preservatives, and fiber.

The nutritional adequacy statement tells whether the food is designed for puppies, adults, seniors, or growth. While the AAFCO establishes feeding trial guidelines, the label doesn't ensure that the food has been tested to determine how a dog thrives on the diet.

THE IMPORTANCE OF WATER

Bulldogs are enthusiastic water drinkers. Just look at the floor around the water dish once your Bulldog has gotten her fill.

To maintain good health and be comfortable, dogs need to remain properly hydrated. All dogs should drink at least $1/4$ cup (59 ml) of water per 2.2 pounds (1 kg) of their body weight every day. Hot weather and heavy exercise increase the need for water by two or three times.

Giving your Bulldog tap water is OK, unless your water source is high in fluoride, chlorine, nitrates, iron, or magnesium, which can be harmful to canines. In this case, filtered water is a healthy alternative. Keep your dog's bowl filled with fresh water every day. To prevent algae and bacteria proliferation, thoroughly clean the bowl daily.

Use a deep stainless steel or stoneware crock-style bowl. These are easy to keep clean, and the water stays cold longer than it does in other kinds of bowls.

Look for dog food that has been certified by the American Association of Feed Control Officials (AAFCO). This organization sets standards with regard to ingredients and additives that are included in pet foods. AAFCO also holds feeding trials to confirm that particular brands of dog food provide a nutritionally complete and balanced meal.

COMMERCIAL FOOD

Walk into any pet supply store and you'll see rows and rows of bags and canned dog food piled high. Kibble, or dry food, is the most popular recipe. Nearly 95 percent of all dog owners feed their pooch kibble. While opening a bag of dry food and scooping some out for your Bulldog's meal couldn't be any easier, some brands may not provide the best diet for her overall health.

Many brands of kibble are labeled nutritionally complete because they contain the required minimum amounts of nutrients. Still, some brands contain the highest-quality ingredients while others do not.

When choosing kibble, avoid brands containing animal by-products. These are ground, rendered, and cleaned slaughtered meat carcass parts, such as necks, feet, undeveloped eggs, bones, heads, intestines, and a small amount of chicken feathers. You'll find animal by-products in lower-grade dog food recipes listed as "beef, chicken, and/or poultry byproducts."

What's a good-quality commercial recipe? Look for a commercial dry food recipe that contains whole meat (chicken, turkey, beef, lamb, or fish). Carbohydrates can include vegetables such as sweet potatoes or complex carbohydrates such as barley or

Your dog's diet must include the proper amounts of protein and fat to support healthy growth and provide energy. If you're feeling confused by the wide variety of dog foods that are available, ask the breeder or your dog's veterinarian for nutritional advice.

quinoa. These cause fewer allergies than corn and wheat.

Low-grade dry food uses lower-quality grain by-products such as brewer's rice, corn, and wheat as fillers because they're inexpensive. Unfortunately, your dog is more likely to have an allergic reaction to these grains.

INGREDIENTS TO AVOID

Inferior dog foods often contain nine ingredients that you should avoid:

1. Butylated hydroxyanisole (BHA) or butylated hydroxytoluene (BHT).

These preservatives prevent spoilage and extend shelf life. However, some studies indicate that they are carcinogenic. Better recipes use vitamin C and vitamin E (mixed tocopherols) as preservatives. Unfortunately, foods with these preservatives don't last as long as foods with BHA or BHT.

2. Ethoxyquin. This preservative is linked to impaired liver and kidney function.

3. Propylene glycol. This liquid is used to prevent the food from drying out, but it may cause central nervous

system impairment and changes in kidney function.

4. Propyl gallate. This antioxidant prevents fats and oils from spoiling, but may cause skin irritation.

5. Coloring agents. Red dye 40 and yellow dye 5 brighten food, but they have been linked to cancer.

6. Phosphoric acid. A clear liquid, phosphoric acid serves as a flavoring agent and an emulsifier that prevents discoloration. It may irritate skin and mucous membranes.

7. Sorbitol. A synthetic sugar substitute used to flavor food, Sorbitol may cause diarrhea and intestinal upset, especially in large quantities.

8. DI-alpha tocopheryl acetate. This synthetic form of vitamin E is not easily absorbed.

FAST FACT

You can always change your Bulldog's diet. But you should do so gradually, over a week or two. Begin by mixing a little of the new food in with her regular diet. Slowly increase the ratio of new to older food.

9. Menadione sodium bisulfate vitamin K$_3$. This synthetic form of vitamin K may irritate mucous membranes.

WET, SEMI-MOIST, AND FROZEN FOOD

Wet food doesn't have as many carbohydrates as dry food, and it contains 72 to 78 percent water. This high percentage of water means that dogs have to eat more of it to obtain adequate nutrition. Wet food, available in cans or foil packages, tastes great because it has more additives and flavor, which explains why most dogs like it. Canned or packaged foods are convenient if you're traveling and your Bulldog is a little picky come mealtime, but once opened any leftover portion must be refrigerated. Wet foods are also more expensive than dry food. Better-quality wet foods contain whole meat, fish, or poultry, as well as vegetables and healthy carbohydrates such as rice, oatmeal, or sweet potatoes.

Most owners use wet food to make dry food more palatable. You should avoid feeding your dog wet food exclusively, however. Not only would it be hard for your dog to get enough nutrition without becoming obese, but canned food tends to stick to teeth and can be a source of dental disease.

Semi-moist food is tasty but expensive. It contains a high percentage of sugar, which leads to dental decay and obesity and isn't the best choice for your Bulldog. This type of dog food can normally be found in

NO-NO FOODS

A few human foods and beverages are dangerous to your Bulldog. Even a small amount of alcohol will cause disorientation and vomiting and can be fatal. Avocado contains persin, a doggy toxin that damages the heart and lungs. Also, an avocado pit can easily become lodged in the intestinal tract, requiring surgical removal. All forms of chocolate and coffee should be avoided, as they contain caffeine and theobromine, cardiac stimulants and diuretics that cause vomiting, rapid breathing, and seizures in dogs.

If your dog consumes between nine ounces and two pounds of grapes or raisins, she will probably suffer vomiting, diarrhea, abdominal pain, lethargy, and acute kidney failure. Don't give your Bulldog any macadamia nuts either. These cause weakness, muscle tremors, and temporary paralysis of the rear legs. Avoid onions, leeks, shallots, scallions, chives, and garlic, which are all toxic to dogs.

Take care when you're baking. Don't leave any yeast dough where your dog can snatch it. Rising yeast dough can lead to rupture of the canine digestive system.

Foods containing Xylitol, an artificial sweetener, are also dangerous for your Bulldog. Ingesting these foods may cause a sudden drop in your dog's blood sugar and lead to liver damage.

Chocolate (left) and macadamia nuts (below) are among the foods that can cause a toxic reaction in your Bulldog.

the refrigerated section of pet supply stores.

Frozen food is available in cooked and raw recipes. You can get it from a pet supply store or by mail order. Owners who want to give their Bulldogs non-commercial food can opt for these recipes. You simply defrost a portion and supplement it with fresh fruits and vegetables.

HOME-COOKED MEALS

You've probably heard the advice not to give your dog table scraps. But people who feed their dogs home-cooked food start with fresh ingredients. The trick to feeding your dog a healthy meal is to avoid giving her any junk food. If it's not good for you, you shouldn't feed it to your Bulldog. Avoid high-fat foods and goodies like donuts, cookies, chips, pizza, pickles, or meals with sauces.

There are advantages and disadvantages to making your dog's food. The biggest drawback is the time required. The biggest benefit is knowing exactly what your dog is eating. You can choose the ingredients according to your Bulldog's needs. If you want to improve your dog's coat, for example, you can increase the fat content.

Protein, such as cooked lean chicken, turkey, duck, beef, lamb, venison, pork, or fish, should make up 30 to 60 percent of the meal. Carbohydrates in the form of cooked grains, such as brown rice, millet, barley, potatoes, rolled oats, or winter squash, should make up another 30 to 60 percent. Vegetables or fruit can make up 10 to 30 percent of the meal. Raw fruit is OK if it is finely chopped. Lightly steam green beans, broccoli, summer squash, cauliflower, carrots, and spinach. Include a calcium and phosphorus supplement. Adult Bulldogs need 500 to 600 milligrams of calcium and 240 to 300 mg of phosphorus per day. Add one or two teaspoons of salmon oil to provide omega-3 fatty acids.

Before whipping up a portion of home-cooked food, make sure it contains well-balanced nutrition. Just giving your Bulldog meat and brown rice isn't enough. She needs all of the ingredients in the recipe in the correct proportions, as well as the supplements.

FAST FACT

Your dog should never be fed bones from cooked chicken, pork, lamb, or fish. These may break and splinter, and their sharp ends can pierce the stomach or intestinal wall or cause an obstruction.

FAST FACT

Veterinarians once believed that senior dogs over seven years of age should eat less protein than they got in their younger years, but that is no longer the consensus. When deciding how much protein to feed your older Bulldog, evaluate how active she is, her overall condition, and her surroundings. Strenuous exercise and extreme weather conditions require more protein and fat in your Bulldog's diet.

A Bulldog weighing 50 pounds (23 kg) should eat about 1 to 1.5 pounds (0.45 to 0.68 kg) of fresh food each day. While this doesn't sound like much, whole food is more digestible and provides more nutrients than commercial recipes.

Once you're familiar with how to design a healthy diet for your Bulldog, you can organize the meals you cook for yourself and save a portion for your pooch. Leftovers can be frozen and saved for future meals.

RAW DIETS

A raw diet excludes not only all commercial dog foods but also all cooked foods. Many owners believe that cooking food at high temperatures destroys vitamins, enzymes, and antioxidants.

The Biologically Appropriate Raw Foods (BARF) diet, created by Dr. Ian Billinghurst, incorporates raw bones and meat, some vegetables, and a few carbohydrates. Raw chicken bones, carcasses, wings, and necks are typically used. If raw meaty lamb, beef, venison, duck, rabbit, pig, or whole fish is more readily available, however, owners can use these sources.

A raw diet is meant to resemble what a dog would eat in the wild. It is often used with dogs that have medical issues such as allergies or arthritis, when no other remedies seem to work. Other benefits that proponents tout include less doggy odor, naturally clean teeth, less stool production, better overall health, and less expense than a commercial food diet.

Diets containing raw chicken or meat do have a few risks. Uncooked chicken or meat can harbor salmonella and E. coli bacteria. While salmonella is mild in dogs, infected dogs can carry the bacteria in the saliva and feces. Using organic certified raw meat raised without antibiotics or hormones is the safest option, and it's best to purchase raw ingredients at their freshest and keep them refrigerated. Unless finely ground, raw bones also pose a health hazard—they can pierce the intestinal tract.

Bulldogs of all ages need appropriate chew toys. Chewing will help scrape plaque off a dog's teeth and keep them healthy. You'll still have to brush your pet's teeth on a daily basis, however.

If you're interested in feeding your Bulldog a raw food diet, discuss this feeding alternative with your veterinarian.

HEALTHY TREATS

It's difficult not to get a kick out of the pure enjoyment your Bulldog shows upon receiving a goody. But that doesn't mean she needs a treat just because she looks at you imploringly. Stay strong and resist the urge to hand out more than a couple extras every day. Treats shouldn't exceed 10 percent of her daily food intake.

Use treats when your dog has done something special or during training. Bulldogs aren't usually picky eaters, but those that are finicky will turn their flat noses up at their regular meals if they know they can successfully beg for treats.

Many treats aren't very good for your Bulldog. Commercial snacks are often loaded with calories your dog doesn't need. Many contain high amounts of sugar, salt, and fat, or they contain ingredients you wouldn't use in your dog's regular meals, such as wheat, corn gluten meal, and ground yellow corn. Tasty tidbits often contain harmful preservatives, food dyes, and artificial additives that can cause allergies or severe tearstaining.

Look at the ingredients and the nutritional analysis on the packages.

Since manufacturers are not required to meet any standardized requirements, select those products that do display what they contain. That way you'll know what your Bulldog is eating. Choose tidbits that contain ingredients you recognize, such as brown rice, oatmeal, turkey, carrots, yogurt, or apples.

If you really want to bring a happy expression to your Bulldog's mug, try giving her cut-up pieces of bananas, apples, melons, or some blueberries. Or give her a few cooked peas, green beans, steamed broccoli, or grated carrots or zucchini. These are the healthiest treats you can give your dog. All vegetables strengthen her immune system and help with digestion of carbohydrates, proteins, and fats.

FEEDING SCHEDULES

When you bring your new Bulldog puppy home at around nine weeks of age, she will need to eat three or four meals a day. By the time she's four to six months old, you can gradually eliminate one meal, until you're feeding her twice a day. Adult Bulldogs should always have two meals a day.

Some people leave food out all day, especially if their dog is a little fussy and doesn't finish it all at one time. This isn't recommended. First of all, dogs that dine at their leisure usually become overweight. Second, you'll have difficulty monitoring how

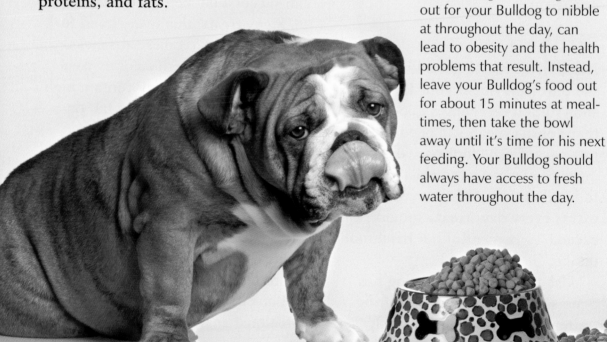

Free feeding, or leaving food out for your Bulldog to nibble at throughout the day, can lead to obesity and the health problems that result. Instead, leave your Bulldog's food out for about 15 minutes at mealtimes, then take the bowl away until it's time for his next feeding. Your Bulldog should always have access to fresh water throughout the day.

much your dog is actually eating, and loss of appetite may signal an illness requiring a trip to the vet.

It's best to feed your dog on a regular schedule—breakfast and dinner. Use a measuring cup so you can regulate the portion size.

OBESITY

An overweight Bulldog is an unhealthy Bulldog. Many veterinarians consider obesity the worst canine health problem.

Between 25 and 50 percent of all dogs are overweight. This condition leads to diabetes, bone and joint diseases, heart and lung diseases, urinary disorders, skin conditions, and some types of cancer. Simply put, extra body weight shortens a dog's life expectancy.

Because many Bulldogs love to eat, avoiding Bulldog bulk can be a constant struggle. A visual inspection can tell you whether your dog needs to shed a few pounds. Look down over the top of her body. You should see an hourglass shape, or a narrowing area behind the rib cage but before the hindquarters. If she's overweight, there won't be any definition. You should also be able to feel your dog's ribs by moving the skin around the rib cage. If you can't feel the ribs, she's carrying too much weight.

To help your overweight Bulldog lose a few pounds, cut back a little on the amount of food you feed her every day. If she seems really hungry, add small pieces of fruit or some cooked or steamed vegetables to her diet. Also increase her exercise. Two 20-minute to 30-minute walks per day are ideal for heart health and weight reduction.

CHAPTER SIX

Keeping Your Bulldog Healthy

Sometimes it takes a village to keep a Bulldog in tip-top shape. Your Bulldog needs you to feed her a healthy diet and to give her plenty of exercise. She also needs a qualified veterinarian with a conscientious office staff to provide good health care.

If you're looking for a veterinarian, ask for referrals from your breeder, rescue coordinator, or friends with dogs. You might also want to

Giving your Bulldog opportunities for regular exercise—two walks each day, as well as time to run and play off-leash in an enclosed area—will keep him fit and healthy.

contact the American Animal Hospital Association (www.healthy-pet.com) and check the Bulldog Club of America's Web site (www.thebca.org) for a list of recommended veterinarians.

When selecting a vet, consider emergency arrangements, facilities, and services. Find out whether the vet attends veterinary conferences to learn about new techniques. Before making a decision, it's a good idea to tour facilities and speak with the vet personally. Beforehand, find out a bit about Bulldog health issues so you can discuss care options with the vet. The two of you should be able to communicate easily. The vet's answers to your questions should be clear, and you shouldn't feel rushed.

Take your new Bulldog to the veterinarian for her first checkup a day or two after you bring her home. Assuming your dog is healthy, the visit should be a positive experience and a chance for your doctor to learn about your dog. Bring a fresh stool sample with you so the vet can check for intestinal parasites. During the routine visit the veterinarian should weigh your dog, listen to her heart and lungs, take her temperature, check her pulse, and examine her coat, skin, eyes, ears, feet, and mouth. The normal temperature for a Bulldog is about 100° to 102°F (38°

Ideally, a prospective veterinary clinic should be a member of the American Animal Hospital Association or a similar organization that inspects and accredits veterinary facilities.

to 39°C). A normal pulse rate at rest can range from about 80 to 140 beats per minute. Typically, smaller dogs have pulse rates at the higher end of that scale.

Discuss an overall health care plan for your Bulldog, including flea, tick, and heartworm preventives, as well as a vaccine schedule. Find out about spaying if your dog is a female, or neutering if your dog is a male. You might also want to review your dog's diet.

SPAYING AND NEUTERING

Unless you are showing your Bulldog, sterilization should be done as soon as possible. Breeding Bulldogs can be a heartbreaking experience. In the best of circumstances Bulldogs seldom have more than three or four puppies, but because Bulldog puppies have the unique anatomy of a large head and shoulders, females seldom deliver their young without needing a cesarean section. This is expensive, costing between $2,000 and $3,000. It can also be life threatening, and inexperienced breeders often lose their females during the birth process.

Another important reason to spay your Bulldog is that it eliminates the possibility of uterine or ovarian cancer and reduces the likelihood of mammary cancer, especially if it's done before your dog's first heat cycle, which usually occurs between 6 and 10 months of age.

Equally good reasons exist for neutering male Bulldogs. If done by one year of age, the procedure eliminates the risks for testicular and prostate cancer. It also reduces dominance and aggressive behavior, the tendency to wander, leg lifting, and mounting.

A final reason for sterilizing dogs is to reduce pet overpopulation. Tens of thousands of dogs are taken to animal shelters every year because their owners no longer want them.

Spaying and neutering procedures are not complicated. Dogs usually go home the same day with only minor discomfort.

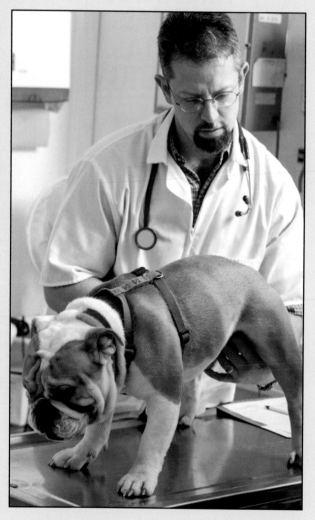

Annual health checkups are recommended for Bulldogs. When your dog is seven or eight years old, he should be examined by the veterinarian at six-month intervals.

Choosing whether or not to spay or neuter your Bulldog is an important decision. The procedure does provide certain benefits with regard to your dog's health and behavior. However, if you plan to show your Bulldog in competitive events like conformation shows, he or she cannot be sterilized.

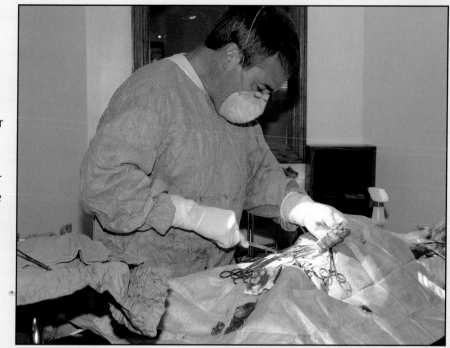

VACCINATIONS AND TITERS

To prevent certain diseases, veterinarians once vaccinated dogs every year. Today the protocol is different. Studies have shown that administering too many canine vaccinations can compromise a dog's immune system. The American Animal Hospital Association recently issued a new set of vaccination guidelines, recommending that vaccines should be administered once every three years.

Puppies need an initial series of core vaccines to protect them from canine diseases. These include distemper, adenovirus, and parvovirus core vaccines at 9 to 10 weeks, 14 weeks, and 16 to 18 weeks, with a booster given at one year. Following this series, the distemper, adenovirus, and parvovirus core vaccines should be administered once every three years.

The one vaccine required by law is the rabies vaccine. You must show proof of rabies vaccination to get a license for your dog, board her in a kennel, or take her on an airplane. The first rabies vaccine should be given at 20 weeks or older. The frequency of required booster shots for rabies varies by state and municipality.

Noncore vaccinations for coronavirus, canine parainfluenza virus, leptospirosis, Lyme disease, and kennel cough (bordetella) should be given when the risk of the disease is significant. Your veterinarian will be able to advise you.

After the initial core vaccines, your veterinarian can measure the levels of protective antibodies already present in the system, called titers, by drawing a blood sample. A high titer count reveals a high level of immunity to the disease, while a low titer count indicates that a dog is still susceptible. Many veterinarians recommend using these titer tests before vaccinating a dog again. Titers are not available for bordetella, parainfluenza, or coronavirus.

EXTERNAL PARASITES

Fleas, ticks, and mites are nasty pests that can drive a dog crazy—and compromise the dog's health. The

WHEN TO SEE THE VETERINARIAN

Take your Bulldog to your veterinarian if the dog:

- is bleeding and you cannot stop it within a few minutes
- has been stung or bitten by an insect and the area is swelling
- has been bitten by a snake
- has been bitten by another animal in a fight
- has been exposed to poison
- has been burned by fire or chemicals
- has sudden swelling or redness
- refuses to eat more than two meals consecutively
- vomits repeatedly
- is unable to urinate or defecate or has blood in her urine or stool
- has persistent diarrhea
- repeatedly scoots her rear end on the ground

- is lethargic
- has a red swollen eye or has crusty or cloudy eyes, excessive tearing, or discharge
- has a dry, chapped, hot, crusty, or runny nose
- has inflamed or bleeding gums, cracked teeth, or foul breath
- has foul-smelling ears
- has red, flaky, itchy, or inflamed skin or repeatedly chews or licks the same areas
- has a dull, dry, brittle, or itchy coat
- has red, swollen, tender, or racked paws or a nail that is torn or bleeding
- is panting excessively, is unable to catch her breath, or makes a wheezing sound while breathing.

If you allow your Bulldog to run and play in wooded, grassy areas where deer roam, be sure to check him for deer ticks (inset) before he comes inside. These tiny parasites are only about the size of a pin head, but they can infect your dog with Lyme disease.

effects of a flea infestation range from skin irritation to severe allergic reactions. Fleas also transmit tapeworms to dogs. To get rid of fleas, treat your dog, her bedding, the entire inside of your house, and the yard. Contact your veterinarian to obtain a spot-on adulticide flea treatment and an oral insect-growth regulator treatment. Be diligent about using them every month.

Ticks are potentially very dangerous. They transmit Lyme disease, Rocky Mountain spotted fever, ehrlichiosis, and tick paralysis. Ticks cling to bushes and inhabit wooded areas. They can leap onto a dog's head, back, or neck when she passes by. If you take your Bulldog walking through wooded or mountainous areas, your dog should be protected with a spot-on flea product that also kills ticks.

Keep the grass short around your home, and remove tall bushes. If you see a tick on your dog, remove it immediately. Use tweezers to gently grasp near the head and pull the tick off. Flush the tick down the toilet. Apply a little hydrogen peroxide to your dog at the site of the tick attachment or bite.

Mites can cause demodectic mange, a condition that mostly affects puppies with weak immune systems. Mites are passed from mothers to their nursing pups during the first days of life. The mites that cause demodectic mange are microscopic, but the condition shows up as red and inflamed areas on the puppy's face, as the mites crowd out the hair follicles and make the hair fall out. Usually the condition resolves itself, but it can be treated with repeated medicated bathing dips.

HEARTWORM

Transmitted by mosquitoes, heartworms are internal parasites that can be deadly to dogs if left untreated. The larvae of these parasites circulate through the dog's bloodstream. In the adult stage, heartworms travel to the right side of the heart. Reaching lengths of up to 12 inches, they can totally engulf that organ.

Once prevalent in the United States only in the South, heartworms are now found in most areas of the country. Your veterinarian can prescribe a preventive medication for you to give your dog once a month.

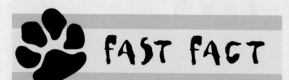

FAST FACT

Roundworms are often passed on to people, especially children. Have your dog checked regularly for intestinal worms.

Heartworm medication can also be used to prevent other internal parasites such as hookworms, roundworms, and whipworms. Roundworms are common in puppies and can easily be killed with medication. Whipworms are more difficult to destroy.

BULLDOG ILLNESSES

Like every breed, Bulldogs are prone to general illnesses as well as certain genetic conditions. To have the best chance of getting a healthy canine companion, buy your Bulldog from a reputable breeder who belongs to the

THE DANGER OF HEARTWORMS

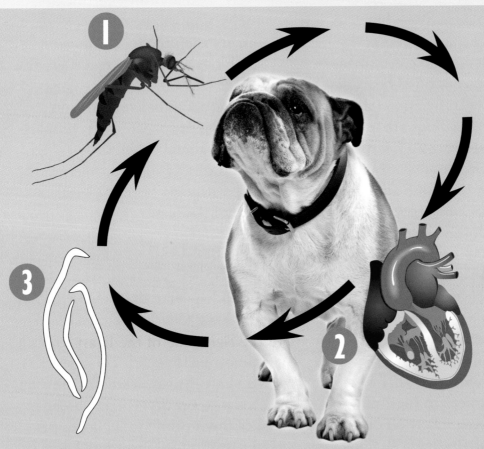

Heartworms are a concern for all dog owners. The graphic above illustrates the cycle of heartworm development. When a mosquito (1) bites an English Bulldog, it can inject microfilaria into his bloodstream. The microfilaria travel through the bloodstream to the heart (2), where they grow into heartworms (3) and multiply, clogging the dog's heart. If left untreated, heartworms can kill.

FAST FACT

The ASPCA maintains a 24-hour Animal Poison Control Center staffed by veterinarians and toxicologists. If you think your Bulldog has ingested a poisonous substance, call the hotline at (888) 426-4435. You may be charged a $60 consultation fee.

Bulldog Club of America. Before breeding two dogs, BCA breeders test them both for a few inherited conditions, such as heritable eye diseases, hip dysplasia, congenital heart disease, and patellar luxation (slipped kneecaps). When dogs are tested, they are identified by a microchip and a DNA profile. Results are recorded with the Canine Health Information Center (CHIC) database.

Even with this testing, there is no guarantee your puppy will grow into a perfectly healthy dog that will live to a ripe old age. However, parents clear of genetic health issues are less likely to produce offspring that will develop an inherited disease. Also, reputable breeders usually offer health guarantees to their puppy buyers covering inherited diseases.

Before purchasing a Bulldog from a breeder, ask if the dog's parents have CHIC identification numbers. The centralized canine health database—jointly sponsored by the AKC/Canine Health Foundation (AKC/CHF) and the Orthopedic Foundation for Animals (OFA)—lists the results of breeders' health testing. You can check the CHIC Web site (www.caninehealthinfo.org) and the OFA Web site (www.offa.org) to locate Bulldogs with CHIC certification numbers that are listed in the OFA database. The OFA Web site also has sample health certificates online so you will be able to recognize what the breeder shows you.

Bulldogs are prone to certain diseases for which no tests are available. That's another reason your Bulldog needs to visit the veterinarian for an annual exam. Often a veterinarian can detect a problem early, when treatments have the best chance of success.

BRACHYCEPHALIC AIRWAY OBSTRUCTION SYNDROME

The Bulldog—like the Boston Terrier, Boxer, King Charles Spaniel, Pekinese, and Pug—is classified as a brachycephalic breed. This means it has a short, broad head. The unusual anatomy of brachycephalic breeds makes them prone to a cluster of upper respiratory disorders known collectively as brachycephalic airway obstruction syndrome (BAOS). These disorders include an elongated soft palate, inflammation of the larynx and trachea, and stenotic nares, or pinched nostrils. Aside from noisy breathing, coughing, snoring, and gagging, symptoms of BAOS include weakness, fainting or collapsing episodes, fatigue, and bluing of the skin and mucous membranes. Overheating is a particular danger because increased panting causes swelling and narrowing of airways.

If you see these signs, take your dog to the veterinarian immediately. To help prevent mild episodes, avoid strenuous exercise and keep your dog cool. During hot and humid weather, keep your dog indoors with the air conditioning on. Having her wear a harness instead of a collar can help keep the trachea from compressing and obstructing her airway. Also, keep your dog at a healthy weight, as being overweight makes breathing more difficult.

Another element of BAOS is hypoplastic trachea, a condition in which dogs are born with an abnormal growth of cartilage in the trachea, constricting the airway. Dogs with hypoplastic trachea generally exhibit problems by five or six months of age.

SKIN ISSUES

Some Bulldogs are prone to skin problems ranging from acne, demodectic mange, interdigital cysts, lick granuloma, and skin fold dermatitis. An omega-3 fatty acid supplement, such as salmon or flaxseed oil, will strengthen your Bulldog's skin.

Pimples pop up on young Bulldogs' chins and abdomens when you least expect them. To treat acne, wash your dog's face every day or rub in some benzoyl peroxide cream twice a day.

If you've ever had a blister between your toes, you know how painful that can be. Imagine how a Bulldog feels when there's a cyst between her toes. Interdigital cysts, which frequently are filled with pus, occur when the little hairs between the toes grow back into the skin. Left untreated, they can become infected. Put your dog in the tub and soak the paw in warm water and Epsom salts. Then dry the paw thoroughly and apply an antibiotic ointment, available from your veterinarian.

When a dog continually licks at a spot on her front or rear leg, it doesn't take long before the spot becomes a raw and painful open sore called a lick granuloma. The constant licking that produces a lick granuloma may be a response to a medical issue, such as allergies, arthritis pain, a fungal infection, or cancer. Or it may have psychological causes, such as separation anxiety, boredom, or stress. Treat the sore by determining the underlying cause and breaking the itch-lick cycle with either a long-acting corticosteroid and a restraint collar or acupuncture. Providing more exercise and additional human or animal companionship may be helpful.

The Bulldog's deep wrinkles make the breed prone to a condition called skin-fold dermatitis. Inside the wrinkles, the friction of skin rubbing against skin, combined with moisture and bacteria, can produce painful lesions and sores. To avoid skin-fold dermatitis, clean your Bulldog's wrinkles—paying special attention to the face and chin—every day.

EYE DISEASES

If you observe your Bulldog rubbing her face on the ground or against furniture, something may be bothering her eyes. Give the veterinarian a call and arrange for an examination.

Cherry eye is a condition in which a red mass protrudes from the corner of the dog's eye. It is caused when a gland in the dog's third eyelid, or nictitating membrane, slips out of place. Treatment involves surgery to replace the eyelid, or surgery to remove the eyelid and gland.

Keratoconjunctivitis sicca, or dry eye, is a common Bulldog problem. It is characterized by itching, burning, or irritation of the eye, or by

Conjunctivitis, which is characterized by redness of the eye's outer layer, or sclera, is a common problem in English Bulldogs. Any time your Bulldog's eyes become obviously red or irritated, take him to the veterinarian. Certain eye conditions can progress to permanent blindness if they are not treated promptly.

light sensitivity. Often the cause is insufficient production of tears. A veterinarian can prescribe drops or an ophthalmic ointment to treat the condition.

Entropion is an inherited eye problem common in Bulldogs. It occurs when the lower eyelid rolls inward, causing the eyelashes to scrape the dog's cornea. Symptoms include tearing, squinting, or a discharge. A veterinary ophthalmologist must surgically repair entropion.

Progressive retinal atrophy (PRA) is another inherited eye disease. It is characterized by abnormal development or premature degeneration of the retina. Affected dogs first lose their night vision. Then their day vision is lost. Blindness occurs as young as six months and as late as eight years of age. There is no treatment. While most Bulldogs don't develop PRA, many reputable Bulldog breeders have their breeding stock's eyes tested annually by a veterinary ophthalmologist as a precaution. Test results are submitted to the Canine Eye Registry Foundation (CERF).

HIP DYSPLASIA

Hip dysplasia is a condition in which the head of the femur—the long bone of the upper leg—doesn't fit tightly into the socket of the hip joint. This results in lameness, pain, and osteoarthritis. Hip dysplasia has a strong genetic component; a puppy is very likely to develop the problem if a parent had it.

Signs of hip dysplasia may be present in puppies as young as five months. These puppies may run with a "bunny hop" gait or display stiffness or pain in the rear legs. Minimizing strenuous exercise while the dog is under two years of age—when the hip and leg bones are still developing—may mitigate the effects of hip dysplasia. While surgery can repair the joint, the procedure is expensive and requires a long recovery.

Hip dysplasia results from a hereditary malformation of the hip bones. This X-ray shows how a dog's left leg (pictured on the right) does not fit properly in the hip socket. The problem can be seen in the other hip joint as well, although it is not as pronounced.

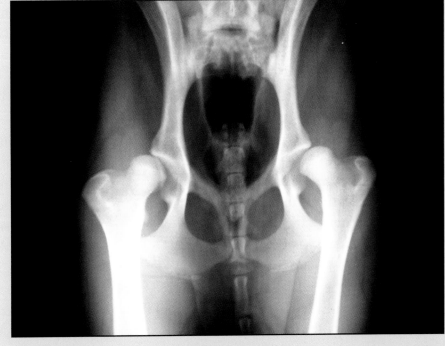

Bulldogs should not be permitted to overexert themselves, especially in warm weather, as members of this breed are prone to overheating because of their short noses. Dogs do not sweat like humans do, so on hot days a Bulldog must pant and drink water to reduce his core body temperature. A dog that is not able to cool himself is at risk for heatstroke, which can be fatal.

A veterinarian can diagnose hip dysplasia with X-rays. These are submitted to either the Orthopedic Foundation for Animals (OFA) or the University of Pennsylvania Hip Improvement Program (PennHIP) for an evaluation. At the OFA, three veterinary radiologists evaluate the X-rays and assign a grade of excellent, good, fair, or fail. The results are compiled in a database.

The PennHIP method uses different radiograph views of the dog's hips and identifies the exact degree of looseness in the joint. Some breeders believe this method is more accurate than the OFA's, but breeders use both evaluations.

When you buy a Bulldog puppy from a breeder, ask to see the parents' OFA or PennHIP certificates. A dog older than two years of age can be certified free of hip dysplasia.

CONGENITAL HEART DISEASES

Bulldogs are prone to a few inherited heart defects, including aortic stenosis and heart murmurs. A veterinarian trained in cardiac diagnosis can detect these and other conditions during an initial examination and a follow-up echocardiogram (ECG).

Aortic stenosis is a partial obstruction to the flow of blood as it leaves the left side of the heart through the aorta, the body's main arterial vessel. The obstruction forces the heart to work harder to pump blood. Eventually this can cause damage to the heart. Dogs with mild aortic stenosis may show no symptoms. In dogs with moderate to severe cases, symptoms include coughing, difficulty breathing, fainting, and heart failure. The condition can be fatal. A veterinarian may prescribe drugs or put the dog on a limited exercise regimen.

Heart murmurs, which are often caused by a leaky heart valve, may be mild or serious. Most disappear by the time the puppy reaches six months of age. Persistent and moderate heart murmurs can be managed with medication. Surgery to repair a bad valve is high risk and frequently unsuccessful.

Bulldogs should be certified clear of cardiac problems before they are bred. Before buying a Bulldog puppy, ask the breeder for a copy of the parents' cardiac-test results.

PATELLAR LUXATION

Patellar luxation, or slipped kneecaps, is a common hereditary disorder. Pups as young as eight weeks may begin to limp and show signs of suffering when the patella (kneecap) moves out of place.

Mild cases seldom require treatment. The kneecap may pop back into place spontaneously, or your veterinarian may be able to move it back. In severe cases, surgery is the only effective treatment.

HEATSTROKE

If the temperature is warmer than 80°F (27°C), Bulldogs can suffer from heatstroke. While dogs with long muzzles are able to exchange heat by panting, flat-faced breeds such as Bulldogs have more difficulty, as there's little room to exhale warm air away from the body.

Signs of heatstroke include heavy panting, deep labored breathing, increased salivation before gums dry out, weakness, confusion, and vomiting or diarrhea. To prevent heatstroke, keep your dog out of the heat and always provide plenty of access to cool, fresh water.

During the summer months especially, exercise your Bulldog in the early morning or in the evening, and watch for signs of heatstroke. Bring plenty of water during all excursions. If you plan to stay outdoors with your dog for an extended period, carry a small tent or shade cloth to provide protection from the sun.

CHAPTER SEVEN

Looking Good

Bulldog aficionados love the breed's cool look and natural charisma. An added benefit is the Bulldog's short, knot-free coat. Bulldogs don't require a lot of grooming to look their best.

Like all breeds, the Bulldog's skin and coat should be regularly bathed and brushed. Your dog's nails should be trimmed once a week. Clean the ears, the tail, and face wrinkles every day. If you neglect to wipe out your Bulldog's dewlaps—the many skin folds hanging from the jaw to the chest—bacteria will collect there, causing irritation and infection. Your Bulldog's teeth need daily brushing as well.

One reason for the Bulldog's popularity is that members of this breed can look good without requiring a lot of grooming time.

USING A TABLE

While most Bulldogs are quite comfortable lying on their side on the bed or the couch while you do the brushing and nail clipping, the job is much easier if you put your dog up on a table. You can spread a rubber-backed plastic tablecloth on top of your picnic or dining table so she won't slide. Or you can purchase a grooming table.

Professional tables come with a range of features—and a range of price tags. At the high end are models with an electronically controlled lift that can retail for a few thousand dollars. A collapsible model that costs around $100 will also get the job done. These tables have a nonslip surface, fold down for storage, and adjust to your height so you don't have to bend over your dog. You can find them in pet supply catalogs, through professional pet grooming supply companies, or on Internet sites.

A handy accessory for your grooming table is a grooming arm and loop. The bottom of the arm clamps onto one end of the table, and the adjustable loop fits around your dog's neck to help hold her steady so you can work with both hands.

When your dog needs medication or ear cleaning, the table will come in handy too. Never leave your dog unattended on any table, as she could easily fall off and become injured.

PLANNING AHEAD

There's nothing complicated about grooming a Bulldog, especially if you set aside a few minutes every day and begin training her to accept the process a few days after bringing her home. Rather than being stressful, the procedure should be a positive experience for both of you.

At the first session expect that your dog may be too fussy and wiggly to receive all of the grooming. Don't worry. Instead, focus on the fact that you're establishing a spruce-up routine and that your dog will relax as she becomes more comfortable with the procedures. Be firm, but patient.

Bulldogs don't require many grooming tools, but it's a good idea to gather everything you might need before beginning your routine. This way you won't have to stop in the middle and leave your dog alone if you forget something. Your supplies should include: a canine toothbrush and toothpaste, cotton strips, ear cleaner, a fine-toothed or flea comb, nail clippers or a nail grinder, a nonslip bathmat, oatmeal-based or therapeutic doggy shampoo and conditioner, petroleum jelly, a rubber brush, a washcloth, and towels.

BRUSHING

The Bulldog's straight, short coat needs a thorough brushing at least once a week and preferably two or three times a week. Brushing distributes the natural oils throughout the skin and removes dander and dirt. When your dog sheds in the spring and fall months, brushing her every day will allow you to catch the dead hair in the brush rather than having it fall on your floor, furniture, and clothing.

Don't use a hard-bristle brush, which can tear your Bulldog's coat. Instead, use a pliable rubber brush with rubber nubs, a rubber-grooming glove, or a slicker brush with flexible metal pins.

Start at your dog's rear. First brush against the direction of the hair growth, then brush with it. Maintain a gentle but

firm touch along the back and toward the tail. Go over the sides, legs, chest, and top of your dog's head. Brush until no more loose hair or dander comes out.

When you're finished brushing, go over your dog's coat with a plastic or metal flea comb. The comb isn't used for flea control, but merely to discover whether your dog has fleas. If you find any of the tiny pests, contact your veterinarian about using flea control products. Also be on the lookout for any ticks that may be hiding around the neck or rear, between the toes, or in the ears. If you find any, remove them immediately. While brushing your dog you should also check her over for any bumps, deep scratches, or broken nails that may need treatment.

If you're not bathing your dog, end the session by wetting a towel and wiping down your Bulldog. For a fragrant finish, spray a little mink oil over your dog's coat. This will give her an extra shine.

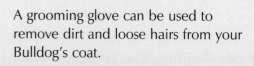

A grooming glove can be used to remove dirt and loose hairs from your Bulldog's coat.

ABC'S OF BATHING

You don't need any special bathing equipment to give your Bulldog a bath, although a hand-held shower attachment makes the job much easier. Another helpful accessory is a mesh drain liner, which will catch dog hair and prevent your drain from clogging. For a quick spot-bath, waterless canine shampoo works wonders when you don't have time for a full soak.

Put a rubber bath mat on the bottom of your tub or shower to prevent your dog from slipping and injuring herself. During warm, but not hot, weather you can even bathe your dog outdoors on the lawn. Wherever you bathe your Bulldog, make it a fun experience, and always be sure to use warm water. Bulldogs hate cold water.

Before putting your Bulldog in the tub, put enough water in the bottom to cover her feet. Once she's in, give her a few minutes to become accustomed to the tub and the water. Start by slowly wetting the neck and sides of her body, working toward the rear. Wet a washcloth in the water and gently wash her face, including her nose and eyes, the outside of her ears, and between the folds and wrinkles of the face and neck.

When bathing your Bulldog, try to keep his head dry until the very end of the bath. Once a dog gets his head wet, he'll want to shake himself dry.

If you're using a concentrated shampoo, pour some of it into a squeeze bottle, add water, and mix. Squeeze a small amount of the shampoo on your dog's neck, along her back and sides, and down the legs.

FAST FACT

The type of shampoo that is best for your Bulldog will depend on the condition of her skin. Veterinarians recommend an oatmeal-based shampoo for dogs with itchy skin, a moisturizing shampoo for dogs with dry skin, an antiseborrheic shampoo for dogs with excessive scale and dandruff, and an antimicrobial shampoo for dogs with damaged skin.

Use the rubber brush to lightly massage the shampoo into the coat. Rinse completely.

Add the conditioner to the coat. Be sure to rinse off the conditioner before towel drying. Soap residue dries out the skin and may cause flaking and itching. Use a damp washcloth to wipe between the toes and between all of the wrinkles. Thoroughly towel dry between the wrinkles, as dampness between the folds may lead to infection. Then dry off the rest of your Bulldog using towels or a hair dryer on the coolest setting.

CLEANING EARS, NOSE, AND TAIL

The Bulldog's characteristic rose ear needs special care. A good habit to get into is to flip up your Bulldog's ears and check inside them each day.

If not cleaned regularly, the ear opening collects dirt and debris, which breed infection.

On a lighter-colored Bulldog, healthy ears should be pink but not bright red, which signals infection. Brindle Bulldogs will have darker-colored ears, but they should not have a red cast either. Ears should not emit a foul-smelling odor, as this is a sign of waxy buildup and infection.

When cleaning your Bulldog's ears, you don't need to worry about hurting her. Unlike the human ear, the canine inner ear is an L-shaped canal that can safely be cleaned before the 90-degree bend. Squirt a little medicated ear cleaner inside each ear opening. Hold the base of the ear on the outside and rub it together a few times, which will loosen the accumulated dirt and debris inside. You should hear a squishing sound. Insert a cotton strip inside the ear as far as possible and

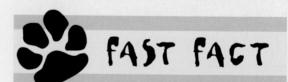

FAST FACT

If your dog is scratching her hair out, she may have allergies, parasites, or a bacterial or fungal skin infection. Your veterinarian can diagnose these conditions.

twist and turn it to wipe out the debris. Never use cotton swabs or anything sharp, as this can injure the ear and doesn't reach all the crevices. Repeat the process until the cotton comes out mostly clean. Although your dog might not like having her ears cleaned, the alternative may be a full-blown ear infection, which is very painful.

Your Bulldog's nose needs regular attention too. Rub a dab of petroleum jelly on her nose to prevent cracking and to keep it soft.

The tail requires daily care as well, or the skin beneath it will become wet and irritated. Use a baby wipe to keep the tail and area around it clean and dry. This should be done several times each day. If you see redness or raw areas under the tail, apply unscented diaper rash cream to keep moisture out of the area until it heals.

WRINKLE AND TEARSTAIN CARE

Those charming facial and neck wrinkles your Bulldog sports need to be cleaned once a day. Use a wet washcloth and some human liquid soap, dog shampoo, or aloe baby wipes to wipe out each wrinkle. Don't forget to wash the wrinkle on top of your dog's nose, the ridges down her cheeks, the deep wrinkles under the eyes, and the furrow on her forehead. Dry thoroughly. If any areas are red and look irritated, apply a little medicated ointment, which is available from your veterinarian.

It is important to clean your Bulldog's wrinkles regularly to prevent skin infections. Soak a washcloth in warm water and antibacterial soap, then carefully clean out the crevices and wrinkles on and around his face. A cotton swab can also be used, as long as you are gentle. Be sure to dry his face and wrinkles completely after you are done.

A good rule of thumb is, if you can hear your Bulldog's nails clicking when he walks on tile, linoleum, or hardwood floors, it's time for the nails to be trimmed.

Some Bulldogs have no trouble with tearstains; others continually manifest this condition. On lighter-colored Bulldogs with lots of wrinkles, the stains are reddish-brown. On darker dogs they're brown. Tearstains have several causes, including ear infections; low-grade bacterial infections in the tear ducts; epiphora, or excess tearing; and thick tears, which can clog up the tear ducts. Artificial dyes and chemicals in commercial dog foods may contribute to thick tears.

Pet supply stores sell several products to erase tearstains. Alternatively, you could make your own paste by mixing 1 tablespoon of hydrogen peroxide, a few drops of Milk of Magnesia, and some cornstarch as a thickener. Apply a little to the stain, but be careful to keep it out of your dog's eyes. It may take a few weeks to lighten the stain. If your dog has chronic tearstains, it's best to take her to the veterinarian to determine the exact cause.

NAIL CARE

Far from mere pampering, keeping your Bulldog's nails short and off the ground is all about health and safety. Her characteristic shuffle or sidewise roll depends upon having strong legs and moderately sized feet with short and stubby toenails.

When a Bulldog's nails are too long, they bear some of the dog's weight, which is painful. Long nails can also tear off and bleed after catching on clothing, carpeting, or outdoor objects.

To keep your Bulldog's nails at an appropriate length, clip them once a week. If you're uncomfortable with the procedure, take your dog to a groomer. But the more practice you have doing it yourself, the easier it gets. Handle your dog's feet every day so she becomes accustomed to the sensation before you begin the actual clipping.

Gently pick up one foot and press lightly on the pad so the nail extends. Using canine nail clippers or an electric nail grinder, take off the pointed tip of the nail. Give your dog a tiny food treat as a reward. Cut a few more nails, but don't worry about finishing all of them at your

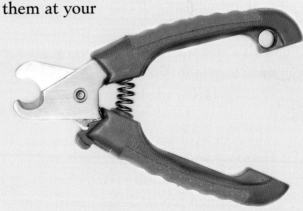

Pet stores sell clippers that you can use to trim your Bulldog's nails.

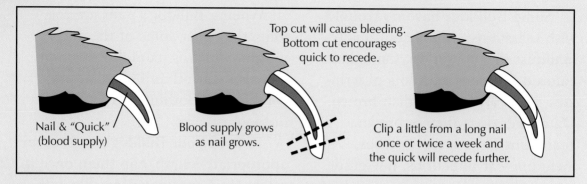

If you're not sure where the quick is located, err on the side of caution when trimming your Bulldog's nails. It is better to leave your dog's nails a little long than to cut the blood vessel, as this will cause pain and bleeding.

first session if your dog begins to get restless.

Many Bulldog fanciers find it easier to use a nail grinder than to use clippers. While it takes a bit longer with the grinder, you can remove a little of the nail at a time and see how close to the quick, or blood vessel, you're coming. With the grinder you can shape the nails and smooth over any rough edges. Regardless of which tool you're using, if you cut a nail too short and it bleeds, apply pressure with a wet washcloth or dab on an anticoagulant, such as styptic powder or cornstarch, to stop the bleeding.

DENTAL CARE

Keeping your Bulldog's teeth and gums healthy requires daily brushing. Like human teeth, doggy teeth can form plaque—a combination of bacteria, saliva, and bits of food—if not cleaned. It takes less than three days for plaque to harden into tartar, which can't be brushed away. Tartar leads to periodontal disease and tooth loss.

Use a toothbrush made especially for dogs or a canine rubber finger brush and canine toothpaste that dissolves in your dog's mouth without rinsing. Dogs usually like the taste of the flavored toothpaste. Put a little toothpaste on your finger and let your dog lick it off. To her, this is like a treat. From there you can progress to putting the paste on a brush.

Begin brushing your dog's teeth after all of her 42 adult teeth are fully developed. Usually this occurs at about six or seven months. With older dogs, begin brushing after a professional cleaning. Stand next to your dog and gently lift up the side of her lip. Quickly align the bristles

A finger brush can be used to keep your dog's teeth clean. Brush every day using a toothpaste specially formulated for dogs. Don't try to save money by using your toothpaste—human toothpastes contain chemicals that can be harmful to your pet, and your Bulldog won't like the minty flavor anyway.

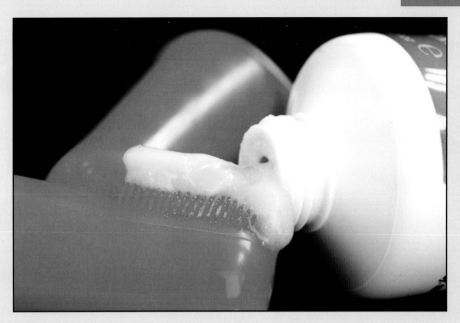

of the brush along the gum line of the upper back teeth and brush from back to front in small circles along the gum line. Continue to the front of your dog's mouth. Repeat on the same side of the mouth with the bottom teeth before brushing the other side of the mouth.

Once every six months to a year, your Bulldog should have her teeth professionally cleaned by the veterinarian. The veterinarian will use an ultrasonic scaling tool to scrape down all of the tartar above and below the gum line.

Some commercial dental toys promise to clean your dog's mouth, but they barely scratch the surface. These toys should never be used as a substitute for regular brushing.

CHAPTER EIGHT

Bulldog Day Out

Your fun-loving Bulldog would much rather accompany you wherever you go than remain at home alone. She is, after all, a natural companion dog.

But while your Bulldog might always be game, you need to make sure she doesn't overdo it trying to keep up with you. Forget about taking your Bulldog with you when you jog, bike, or swim. Bulldogs are simply not built to be good runners, and they can't swim.

A walk in the morning and in the evening provides ideal exercise for your Bulldog. Don't take her out for exercise right after she eats, and remember not to take her out when

Your Bulldog will be happiest if exercise time means time spent with you.

the temperature is above 80°F (27°C).

Walking your Bulldog in winter presents special challenges as well. After a romp in the snow, be sure to wipe icy particles off her feet. Many people use lime rock salt and calcium chloride on sidewalks. If your Bulldog licks her feet after walking through these chemicals, she may experience vomiting and diarrhea. Be on the alert for antifreeze on the ground. Don't let her walk through it or lap it up. When ingested, antifreeze can be fatal.

If you're participating in dog sports, even on cooler days, bring along an exercise pen with a shade cloth or a small tent to shield your dog from the sun. Pack cold water from home, a collapsible water bowl, and a towel soaked in water and stored in an ice chest. While your dog is waiting for her turn to compete, or to cool her off quickly, spread the cold wet towel on the ground and let her stand on it. Dogs perspire through the pads of their feet and their noses. Another way to bring down her body temperature is to apply a cold wet towel against her inner thighs, on her abdomen, and in the armpits.

Never leave your dog in the car when it's warm! On a 73°F (23°C) day, the temperature inside a closed car can reach 120°F (49°C) in 30 minutes. On a 90°F (32°C) day, the temperature can reach 160°F (71°C) in less than 15 minutes. High temperatures will cause heatstroke, which can kill your Bulldog.

OUTDOOR ACTIVITIES

Even if your Bulldog is not the best athlete, there are plenty of ways the two of you can share some fresh-air fun. Take your Bulldog for a stroll at a garden center, browse through an outdoor arts and crafts festival, or have lunch at a dog-friendly café. Let her nudge a soccer ball around the yard. Anything not too strenuous that gets your Bulldog up and moving around makes her healthy and happy.

Many dog owners enjoy taking their canine companions to a dog park. If you've never done so, however, there are a few things you should know. Not all dogs like meeting new dogs, and some respond aggressively. Before taking your Bulldog to an unleashed area, visit the park without your dog to see if you and your dog would feel safe and comfortable there. Familiarize yourself with the rules and see how the park is organized. As long as your Bulldog is safe, she should appreciate getting out of the house, seeing new sights, hearing new sounds, and meeting new friends.

CANINE GOOD CITIZEN

Once your dog has some preliminary training under her paws, consider earning a Canine Good Citizen (CGC) title. The program is sponsored by the AKC. To prepare your dog for the CGC test, you can enroll her in a class, or you can train her yourself.

Before a dog takes the CGC test, the AKC requires owners to sign the Responsible Dog Owners' Pledge. You agree to take care of your dog's health, safety, exercise, training, and quality of life. Cleaning up after your dog in public places and never letting your dog infringe on the rights of others is also your responsibility.

To pass the CGC test, your dog must: allow a friendly stranger to approach, sit quietly and allow the person to pet her, allow someone to

CHILDREN AND BULLDOGS

While there are always exceptions, most kids and Bulldogs go together like peanut butter and jelly. With parental supervision, the pair can become devoted, lifelong friends. It's no surprise, then, that your children will want to hold the leash when you walk the dog or even beg you to let them take the dog out by themselves. If your children are less than 10 years of age, always supervise them. Instruct them on how to react when another dog approaches. Bulldogs are strong and can easily pull a small child into oncoming traffic or up against a menacing dog.

Try purchasing a leash with two handles, or attach a second leash to your dog's collar for your child to hold. As your child grows and begins to understand how much control it takes to walk the dog, you can let the child hold the leash, but always accompany him.

If your child wants more hands-on participation with your dog, show him how to teach your dog some tricks indoors. Training your Bulldog to shake hands or roll over takes time and patience, but the results are sure to please any little one. A child can also assist with feeding and grooming chores.

brush her lightly, walk politely on a loose lead beside you, and walk through a crowd and closely pass at least three people. Your Bulldog will also have to: sit and stay down on a 20-foot-long line while you leave and return, come when you call her, behave politely around other dogs, not react to two distractions, and stay with someone without whining, barking, or pulling while you go out of sight for three minutes.

If your Bulldog growls, snaps, bites, attacks, or attempts to attack anyone, she will fail.

AGILITY

Agility is a canine sport in which dogs—directed by their human handlers—navigate an obstacle course while racing against the clock. Agility competitions are popular because they are fun for both dogs and their handlers. Developed in England in the 1970s, the sport was recognized by the AKC in 1994.

Any AKC-registered dog can compete in agility. The United States Dog Agility Association (USDAA) and the North American Dog Agility Council (NADAC) also sponsor agility competitions. After successfully competing in several trials, your Bulldog can earn Novice, Open, Excellent, and Master titles.

Bulldogs aren't naturals at agility trials, and training a Bulldog to compete in this sport can be difficult. Still, some Bulldogs seem to relish the competition, and your pet may be one of them. You'll have the most success if you have built a strong bond with your dog before you begin training for this sport. Make sure your Bulldog consistently obeys basic commands like "sit," "stay," and "come" before working on more advanced skills. Classes devoted to agility training are available in most cities, or there are many training books, videos, and DVDs that you can use as resources if you'd prefer to train your Bulldog without professional help.

CANINE MUSICAL FREESTYLE

She may have two left feet, but if you think your Bulldog can't dance, think again. Along with their handlers, Bulldogs are capable of performing a choreographed program to the delight of onlookers. Using music and intricate movements to show off teamwork, canine musical freestyle is a popular tail-wagging activity for all breeds.

Dancing with dogs to music takes time, patience, and practice to perfect. But the sport challenges your dog's thinking skills and can be a joy to both of you. While

A young Bulldog clears an agility obstacle.

Bulldogs on the dance floor may not look so light on their paws, you can't convince them they're not having fun once they start rocking out.

To get started, locate classes in your area. You'll need to select a musical composition and a simple costume for you and your dog. Then you have to choreograph a routine. Your performance may consist of obedience steps, dressage movements, tricks, and any new steps you can dream up.

Canine musical freestyle competitors are scored on enthusiasm, degree of difficulty of the movements, and musical interpretation. The World Canine Freestyle Organization (WCFO) and the Canine Freestyle Federation (CFF) sponsor freestyle events and have rules and guidelines you'll need to follow.

OBEDIENCE

Once your dog knows the obedience basics—sit, stay, down, and come—she can perfect her skills in competitive obedience. In obedience trials, dogs begin with a perfect 200 score and have points deducted if they fail to perform a series of exercises correctly.

JUNIOR SHOWMANSHIP

If your child has a hankering to get into the show ring with the family Bulldog, consider Junior Showmanship competition. Sponsored by the AKC, Junior Showmanship is open to children who are at least 9 years old but less than 12. Dogs must be at least six months old, AKC registered, and owned by the child or a member of the child's family. Unlike conformation-show dogs, dogs that participate in Junior Showmanship may be spayed or neutered.

In Junior Showmanship, young dog enthusiasts are judged on how well they present and handle their canine companions. The activity provides a great opportunity for kids to spend quality time with their dogs and to learn good sportsmanship. Before competing, juniors must apply for an AKC junior number.

Training classes for Junior Showmanship are available in most communities. In these classes, children learn the finer points of the sport. They also learn how to practice with their dog.

Bulldogs are capable obedience competitors and can easily achieve the 170 points required to earn the AKC's basic Companion Dog (CD) title. After reaching that milestone, dogs may advance to the levels of Companion Dog Excellent (CDX), Utility Dog (UD), and Utility Dog Excellent (UDX). The United Kennel Club offers the same titles.

To prepare your dog for obedience competition, choose a class that trains dogs for the obedience show ring, and set aside time to practice

THE COSTS OF COMPETITION

If you decide to get involved in competition sports with your Bulldog, the annual cost of caring for your dog will skyrocket, as you add on the following expenses:

Entry fees: $20 to $30 for each class entered. Depending on which sports and how many you compete in with your dog, entry fees for a show or trial can run from $20 to $100, or more.

Transportation: Fuel for your car or motor home to drive to shows within driving distance, and plane fare for important shows farther from home, such as the Bulldog Club of America's annual National Specialty show.

Lodging: Hotel or motel rooms range from $80 to several hundred dollars a night, depending on quality, location, and whether or not the pet fee charged by the hotel is refundable. At some events, participants are permitted to camp on the show grounds. If you own a motor home or camping trailer, this option usually costs from $15 to $50 a night.

Meals away from home: Budget appropriately, depending on your appetite and tastes.

Handler's fees: $100 to $600 or more per show. Hiring a professional handler to exhibit your Bulldog in conformation events, instead of handling him yourself, can increase your dog's success in the show ring, but the cost of earning those awards will increase as well.

Photographs of wins: When your dog wins at a show, captures a title, or earns a perfect score, you will want to get a photograph to remember the day. Sponsoring clubs arrange to have one or more professional photographers on site at the show to provide that service to exhibitors. Dog show photographers generally charge between $25 and $35 per print.

between classes. Even if you don't intend to compete, attending competitive classes with your Bulldog will teach your Bulldog everything you might want her to know.

RALLY-O

Rally obedience—or Rally-O, as fans like to call it—is less structured than competitive obedience. It is tailor-made for Bulldogs. In this sport, dog and handler teams move at their own pace through a course consisting of 10 to 20 stations, depending on the skill level. At each station is a sign with instructions, such as "dog must sit at heel" or "reverse direction." When the dog has completed the specified action, the judge gives the "forward" command, and the dog and handler proceed to the next station. Unlike the rules for competitive obedience, which require silence between exhibitors and their dogs, in Rally-O handlers may communicate with their dogs by clapping hands, talking, or whistling.

Bulldogs compete at all three levels of competition: Novice, Advanced, and Excellent. Dogs remain on leash in Novice but are off leash in the Advanced and Excellent levels.

SHOWING YOUR DOG

No doubt you think your Bulldog is the most gorgeous creature on the face of the earth. Surely if a judge ever saw her in a show ring, she would win Best in Show. Take a deep breath. Before you get too carried away and plunge headfirst into the competitive world of conformation, there are a few things you should know.

Originally the purpose of dog shows was to display breeding stock, so dogs cannot be spayed or neutered. To compete in the show ring, you'll need a well-bred, AKC-registered Bulldog that exudes personality and has show-quality attributes. At a show the judge evaluates how closely a dog matches its breed standard.

Written by the national breed club and approved by the AKC, the breed standard is a description of the ideal dog's body structure, movement, and temperament. It takes a special dog to become a champion.

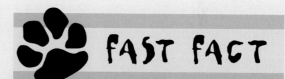

FAST FACT

The famous Westminster Kennel Club dog show, which is televised each year from Madison Square Garden in New York City, is the second oldest continuously held annual sporting event in the United States. The first show was held in 1877, two years after the inaugural running of the Kentucky Derby.

An elderly woman meets a Bulldog at an Ohio nursing home. If you think your well-trained pet would make a good candidate for therapy dog work, consider joining an organization like Therapy Dogs International or the Delta Society.

Before exhibiting your Bulldog, you'll need to train her how to stand still for the judge's examination, how to run at a trot beside you while she's on a leash, and how to turn on the charm to win blue ribbons. Shows are held on many weekends throughout the United States. Along the way you'll meet other Bulldog fanciers and learn about the breed. Showing your dog is a fun, exciting hobby that requires time, patience, dedication, and expense. For more information on show rules and regulations, contact the American Kennel Club and the Bulldog Club of America.

THERAPY DOG

Bulldogs are first-class nurturers. Training yours to be a therapy dog can be tremendously rewarding.

Bulldog therapy dogs turn on the charm in a variety of therapeutic settings. They bring comfort to trauma survivors and rescue workers, greet

the elderly, and befriend the disabled. Whether they're wearing a cowboy costume or rolling over to play dead, count on a Bulldog to liven up any room.

Sometimes they are a vital part of a treatment program and work in pet-assisted therapy programs. As part of her rehabilitation after an accident, for example, one patient worked to regain the use of her hand by reaching up to give a Bulldog a cookie. Although Bulldogs are too big to fit on a patient's lap, either in a wheelchair or on a bed, they can be taught to lift their paws so patients can reach them for petting.

Before going into a facility as a therapy dog, your Bulldog must know basic obedience commands and be confident around strange noises and hospital equipment. Having a few tricks in her repertoire will add to the joy she brings. Therapy dogs must have a health screening, be current on their vaccinations , and be certified with a pet therapy organization such as Therapy Dogs International (www.tdi-dog.org) or the Delta Society (www.deltasociety.org). Therapy dogs must be bathed and brushed before every visit, and their nails should be trimmed.

CHAPTER NINE

Going Sightseeing

Getting away from it all doesn't have to mean leaving your Bulldog behind. Today many vacationers take their loyal companions along for the ride. The adventurous Bulldog doesn't want to miss a move and is ready, willing, and able to go where you go.

Before you hit the road or fly the friendly skies with your four-footed day-tripper, it's vital to plan ahead for your dog's safety and comfort. Taking her special temperature needs in mind, decide if you should pack your Bulldog up with you at all. Ask your veterinarian if your Bulldog will need any new vaccinations to protect her where you're going.

If your dog is well socialized and accustomed to seeing new sights and

With the proper advance planning and preparation, there is no reason your Bulldog can't accompany you on family vacations or trips.

hearing unusual sounds, she'll easily adapt to changing scenery, different situations, and a flexible schedule. If, on the other hand, she's never been away from home, a hectic travel schedule might be stressful.

To introduce your dog to the travel experience, start taking her on short car rides, lasting 10 or 20 minutes. Visit public places, such as outdoor shopping centers or cafés where you'll encounter people and other dogs, and walk your dog around on a leash several times a week. Make the experience fun, so your Bulldog looks forward to becoming a gadabout. If the only time your dog goes anywhere is to visit the veterinarian, she's going to hate getting in the car. So even if you don't plan on traveling with her, take her on errands with you.

In the beginning your Bulldog may experience symptoms of motion sickness. If so, don't feed her a regular meal two hours before the next outing. To help soothe her stomach, give her a few gingersnap cookies or a tablespoon of honey an hour before leaving. To reduce carsickness, leave the window next to her down a little so she has fresh air. If she's in a crate, make sure the crate is facing forward. If your Bulldog is extremely anxious in the car, drive her down the street and back again as frequently as possible so she becomes accustomed to the motion.

It's unsafe to let your Bulldog ride in the back of an open pickup truck. A dog will have trouble keeping his footing, and dangerous objects or insects can fly into his eyes or ears and cause injury. Many states require dogs riding in truck beds to be cross-tethered with a special restraint. The safest ride is inside a crate inside the truck's cab.

WEAR IDENTIFICATION

No matter what mode of transportation you choose for your Bulldog, make sure she's wearing a current identification tag firmly attached to her collar at all times. If you ever become separated from your dog while you're away from home, there's a good chance that anyone who finds her can help reunite you.

Printed legibly on your dog's ID tag should be your name, current address, and home, work, and cell phone numbers, along with the date of your dog's most recent rabies vaccination. If you're traveling to a destination, you can add a temporary ID tag with the name and phone number of the person or hotel you're planning to visit. ID tags that come with a USB port are also available. They can be plugged into any computer to reveal your dog's identification.

For a second form of identification, ask your veterinarian to microchip your dog. A canine ID microchip—about the size of a grain of rice—is inserted via a painless injection under the skin between your dog's shoulder blades. Each microchip is listed in a national database and has an individual number, which matches up to the owner's name, address, phone number, and emergency contact information. A microchip can reunite you and your Bulldog if her collar falls off.

Your Bulldog should have a sturdy collar with an identification tag. The collar can also hold any other tags that local laws require your pet to carry, such as proof of a rabies vaccination or a local dog license. Printing the phrase "needs medication" on a dog's identification tag can encourage the prompt return of a lost pet.

To read the microchip, shelter employees and veterinarians pass a handheld scanner over the dog. Although microchips are designed to remain with the dog throughout her lifetime, sometimes they migrate and cannot be detected by a scanner. Before a trip it is therefore a good idea to take your dog to the veterinarian's office to make sure the microchip is still readable.

Global positioning systems are another option for dog owners who want to ensure that their canine companion doesn't get lost. A small device attaches to your dog's collar and sends a signal to your cell phone or computer informing you of your dog's location.

BULLDOG TRAVEL BAG

Before the day of your departure, pack a bag of things your Bulldog will need for her outing. She'll appreciate a few of her favorite toys, some non-perishable treats, and her blanket. Remember to include any medication she requires. You may need protection against fleas and ticks where you're going, so give your veterinarian a call for preventive medications if your dog isn't already taking them.

It's a good idea to store a copy of your Bulldog's veterinary records, including her proof of vac-

cinations, in her bag too. This information will come in handy if your dog becomes ill and an out-of-town veterinarian needs to know your dog's medical history before providing treatment. Include a few recent photos of her in case she becomes lost.

Be sure to take enough food to last throughout your trip. You may not be able to find the commercial brand she's accustomed to eating in a different city, and an abrupt change in diet can cause intestinal upset. The last thing you want while you're away from home is a sick dog. Don't forget food and water dishes. For frequent trips consider purchasing collapsible bowls.

A few grooming essentials, including dog towels, canine waterless shampoo, and her brush will come in handy for a quick cleanup. Also pack her toothbrush and toothpaste. Include an extra collar and leash in case the others break, a cooling vest, and a shade cloth or netting. Be a responsible dog owner and supply your own plastic bags for picking up your dog's eliminations. If you're staying in a hotel or motel on your trip, it's not a bad idea to carry some pet stain remover with you in case your dog has a bathroom accident in the room.

FIRST-AID KIT

Don't even think of leaving home without a doggy first-aid kit. Hopefully you'll never need to use it. But if an unforeseen situation does arise, you'll be prepared.

Your kit should include antibiotic ointment, antiseptic and antibacterial cleansing wipes, Benadryl, bug repellant, a canine first-aid manual, cotton-tipped applicators, ear cleaner, emergency phone numbers of your veterinarian and emergency clinic, gauze pads, human sunscreen, hydrogen peroxide, an instant cold compress or ice pack, Kaopectate or Pepto-Bismol tablets or liquid, latex gloves, lubricating jelly, a medicine dropper, nail clippers, self-adhering bandages, a small notebook and pen, small scissors, a soft muzzle, sterile saline eyewash, a thermometer, and tweezers.

Check your supplies regularly. Replace items after expiration dates.

ROAD TRIP

Unfortunately, accidents happen. Whether your dog rides shotgun in the car with you for a few blocks or across the country, she needs to be buckled in or crated. If you're ever hit, an unrestrained 50-pound Bulldog can become a dangerous projectile and slam into the windshield, the back of the seat, or another passenger. Dogs should never ride loose in the back of an open pickup truck without being cross-tethered.

If a wire crate fits in your car, this is a perfect place for your

EXITING THE CAR SAFELY

When you take your dog out of the crate or unlock her doggy seat belt harness, clip on her leash before opening the car door. This gives you some control if your dog decides to take off. To prevent your Bulldog from wandering away from you when your back is turned, even for an instant, or from pushing past you the minute the car door is opened, train her not to go beyond a specific point until you give her permission.

Before you open the door, tell her, "sit" and "stay." Give her a super special food treat when she listens to your command. When you're ready for her to exit, say, "OK," and make a big fuss over her when she obeys.

Bulldog. This type of crate permits air to flow around your dog and keep her cool, and she can move around, yet she's protected. Once you crate train your dog at home, the transition to riding in a crate in the car comes easy. Another safety alternative is a doggy seat belt harness, which hooks into your car's seat belt system. If you use an elevated dog booster seat that connects to a harness and the seat belt, the dog can see out the window.

For dogs that don't get carsick, keep the windows either closed or opened just enough for a nose to stick out. Your Bulldog might like to hang her head out of the window, but dangerous debris can fly into her eyes, ears, and nostrils.

Your travel plans during the day should include stopping about once every three to four hours to give your dog a potty break and a chance to stretch her legs. If you're driving through the night, you can probably go longer, as your dog will most likely be catching up on her sleep. Be sure to clean up your dog's mess at the rest stop and dispose of it properly.

AIR TRAVEL

Taking your Bulldog on an airplane requires detailed planning and an advance reservation. Airlines have strict rules about accepting dogs, and

FAST FACT

Your Bulldog should not be tranquilized before you travel. She needs to be awake to shiver or pant if she has to regulate her body temperature.

there are some risks involved in canine air travel, especially with flat-faced breeds that have breathing issues, like the Bulldog.

Before making your airline reservations, check online or call the airline to learn about its pet travel policies. Airlines permit only a limited number of dogs per flight in the cargo section of the plane, and many do not take dogs at all during the summer months. Also expect to pay almost as much for your dog to travel with you as you pay for your fare.

If you do decide to fly with your canine jetsetter, select a nonstop flight so you don't have to worry about her changing planes. Also choose a flight that departs and arrives in the morning or the evening, when it's cooler. You'll need a health certificate and a valid rabies certificate from your veterinarian within 10 days of departure. The certificate states that the veterinarian has examined your dog and that she's healthy.

Airlines do not accept wire crates. Your Bulldog must fly inside a hard-sided, airline-approved crate. It has to be large enough for her to lie down in a natural position, turn around, and stand up or sit erect without her head touching the top.

The crate must be ventilated on opposite sides and have exterior rims and knobs to permit airflow. It must contain shredded paper or a dog blanket to absorb any accidents, and it must be clearly labeled with your name, home address, home phone number, and destination contact information. The door must close securely, but not lock, in case of an emergency. "Live Animal" stickers in one-inch letters must be on the crate's top and on at least one side.

On regular airlines, Bulldogs must travel in the baggage compartment. Pet Airways, which flies out of select U.S. cities, transports dogs and cats inside the cabins of its planes.

Sometimes the airlines will supply these. The crate must have plastic dishes for food and water attached inside the crate door.

Do not feed your dog for six hours prior to your flight. She may have water, however. When you land, give your dog some fresh drinking water. She'll be thirsty!

OVERNIGHT LODGING

If you need to stay overnight in a hotel or motel room, don't leave home without making reservations, as many places don't allow dogs. According to the American Hotel and Lodging Association, only 35 percent of all hotels welcome pets.

Some pet-friendly establishments pamper canine guests with oversized pillows, water bowls in the room, and gourmet dog biscuits. Others charge an extra pet fee and have strict pet rules. When you check in, ask if there are designated potty areas, and of course make sure to clean up after your dog.

When you enter your room, check the floor—especially beneath the bed—for any small objects that your Bulldog might accidentally swallow. Remember that you are a guest in the inn. Don't let your dog chew or tear the linens, carpeting, or furniture.

If your Bulldog has a bathroom accident in the room, clean it up with pet stain remover. Some establishments will charge an extra fee when you check out if the bedspread has dog hair or slobber on it, so it's best to bring an extra sheet to lay over the bedspread if your dog sleeps on the bed with you. Never leave your dog alone in the room because she may bark and disturb other guests.

CHAPTER TEN

Caring for Your Senior Bulldog

Just like people, Bulldogs develop various ailments as they age. Unfortunately, Bulldogs can begin to age in what seems like the blink of an eye. By seven or eight years of age, your Bulldog will be considered a senior dog. There are steps you can take to make his senior years as comfortable as possible. Simply pay attention to the physical changes he's undergoing, and deal with them as they arise. This can make your Bulldog's later years as fulfilling as every other period of his life.

Like you, your Bulldog will be prone to arthritis as he ages. And like you, too, he may benefit from over-the-counter remedies such as a glucosamine/chondroitin formulation that works as a joint lubricant. Ask

The average life span for an English Bulldog is eight to ten years.

your vet if this type of treatment is right for your Bulldog.

Bulldogs seem especially prone to another ailment of aging—corneal ulcers. These are ulcers that appear on the surface of the dog's eye and can cause blindness if not treated promptly. Remember to check your Bulldog's eyes thoroughly every few weeks, especially as he ages.

When you're brushing or bathing your elder Bulldog, run your hands over his body to make sure he's not developing any lumps or bumps. Unfortunately, the senior years are the time when most cancers develop in dogs. Report any suspicious growths to your veterinarian as soon as possible.

Remember, too, to check your Bulldog's teeth and gums. As he ages, gingival hyperplasia may appear. This disease causes the gums to grow over the teeth and can be quite unpleasant for your dog. You can avoid it with regular tooth brushing.

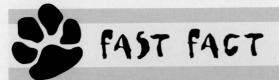

FAST FACT

It's best not to introduce a new puppy into a home with an elderly Bulldog. As the new dog matures, she may become aggressive and try to dominate the weaker, older dog.

FAST FACT

Some elderly Bulldogs will suffer from old-dog syndrome, also known as cognitive dysfunction syndrome. This is the canine equivalent of senility.

Another symptom of aging in some Bulldogs is incontinence. Try not to let your canine pal's sudden puddles around the house upset you, because he'll already be upset enough for both of you. Just give him additional opportunities each day to relieve himself outdoors—almost as if he were a puppy again—and his accidents can be kept to a minimum.

When your Bulldog reaches his senior years, your veterinarian will likely recommend periodic blood work and extra exams. These procedures can help detect any developing kidney or liver problems, heart disease, adrenal disorders, or cancer. All are common problems in aging dogs. As in humans, if these problems are caught early, treatment is easier and the prognosis is better.

NUTRITION

If you've kept your Bulldog fit and trim in his younger years, he should move into his senior years without gaining too much extra weight.

Keeping strict control of your dog's food intake is not always easy, however. Dogs have a knack for finding food, and if they find it, they eat it. That includes food off kids' plates and out of the cat's bowl, not to mention the treats and snacks he might get from family members. So if you find that your Bulldog has become a heavy geriatric, make sure he slims down for his own health and comfort. Excess weight, especially in the senior years, puts additional stress on vital organs and joints, shortening a dog's life.

Reducing your Bulldog's weight may be as simple as just serving him smaller meals now that he's older. Also, there are quality senior dog foods on the market that are lower in fat. If he'll eat raw vegetables, they will provide bulk and nutrition, making your dog feel full, without being full of calories.

As dogs age, their metabolism changes and they don't absorb vitamins and minerals from food as well as they once did. Many older Bulldogs, therefore, benefit from supplements. Some Bulldog owners find that extra vitamins C and E, along with calcium, essential fatty acids like fish oil, and even a kelp or seaweed formula can increase their pets' vitality in old age. Check with your vet or research pet supplements for aging dogs to see what might be helpful for your Bulldog.

EXERCISE

Even though your dog is older, he still needs regular exercise. Exercise will help to prevent your Bulldog from gaining weight and will keep him engaged in life. Even though he may not be as frisky as he once was, your Bulldog will still be curious about what's going on in

It is normal for a Bulldog to have less energy as he ages.

Even though your senior Bulldog may be slowing down physically, he'll still need daily exercise to remain fit and trim.

his neighborhood. So daily walks, at a pace your older Bulldog can manage, will be a pleasure you both can still savor. Keep an eye on his stamina, though, and head for home when it appears that he's getting fatigued.

Old age is, however, the time to eliminate strenuous running and jumping games with your dog. These can put an unnecessary strain on his heart and his joints. Also, avoid temperature extremes: take your Bulldog for walks when it's not too hot or too cold outside.

SAYING GOOD-BYE

Eventually, inevitably, you and your dear friend will have to part. What can be even more difficult, emotionally, is that you may have to decide when it's time for your loyal companion to die. Unless your Bulldog dies peacefully and suddenly at home, it is very likely that he'll have to be euthanized to spare him

Photos of your pet Bulldog in happier times can help ease the pain of his passing.

the pain and suffering of dying slowly from disease. As difficult as this decision will be, you owe it to him.

It might help to think of it this way. Your Bulldog has trusted you for everything all his life—for nourishment, for fun, for a warm place to sleep, and for love. If he had a say in the matter, he would surely trust you to decide his end. Trust yourself. You'll know when disease or injury is robbing your friend of his enjoyment of life and of your company. If no

recovery is possible, it's time. If he can no longer move around without great pain, or if he's no longer eating, it's time. If you want, spend a final weekend with him, so that family members can share time with him, love him, and say good-bye.

The final trip to the veterinarian's office will be very emotional, but try to stay composed for your dog's sake. He won't want to see you upset. The actual process of euthanasia is painless for the dog. The vet will usually administer a sedative first, so your proud friend will fall asleep. Then an overdose of anesthesia is administered, and the dog's heart simply stops beating.

It's perfectly natural to grieve after such an event. Let your grief run its course. Once you've come to terms with your loss, and you feel that you are ready, perhaps you'll want to start looking for a new Bulldog puppy.

Organizations to Contact

American Animal Hospital Assn.
12575 West Bayaud Ave.
Lakewood, CO 80228
Phone: 303-986-2800
Fax: 800-252-2242
E-mail: info@aahanet.org
Web site: www.aahanet.org

American Kennel Club
8051 Arco Corporate Dr., Suite 100
Raleigh, NC 27617
Phone: 919-233-9767
E-mail: info@akc.org
Web site: www.akc.org

Association of Pet Dog Trainers
150 Executive Center Dr., Box 35
Greenville, SC 29615
Phone: 800-738-3647
Fax: 864-331-0767
E-mail: information@apdt.com
Web site: www.apdt.com

The Canadian Kennel Club
89 Skyway Ave., Suite 100
Etobicoke, Ontario, M9W 6R4
Canada
Phone: 416-675-5511
Fax: 416-675-6506
Web site: www.ckc.ca/en

Delta Society
875 124th Ave., NE
Suite 101
Bellevue, WA 98005
Phone: 425-226-7357
E-mail: info@deltasociety.org
Web site: www.deltasociety.org

Humane Society of the U.S.
2100 L St., NW
Washington, DC 20037
Phone: 202-452-1100
Fax: 301-548-7701
Web site: www.hsus.org

The Kennel Club of the U.K.
1-5 Clarges St.
London W1J 8AB
United Kingdom
Phone: 0870 606 6750
Fax: 020 7518 1058
Web site: www.thekennelclub.org.uk

National Association of Dog Obedience Instructors
PMB 369
729 Grapevine Hwy.
Hurst, TX 76054-2085
E-mail: corrsec2@nadoi.org
Web site: www.nadoi.org

National Association of
Professional Pet Sitters (NAPPS)
17000 Commerce Parkway, Suite C
Mt. Laurel, NJ 08054
Phone: 856-439-0324
Fax: 856-439-0525
Web site: www.petsitters.org

National Dog Registry
P.O. Box 51105
Mesa, AZ 85208
Phone: 800-NDR-DOGS
Web site: www.nationaldogregistry.com

North American Dog Agility
Council (NADAC)
P.O. Box 1206
Colbert, OK 74733
E-mail: info@nadac.com
Web site: www.nadac.com

North American Flyball
Association (NAFA)
1400 West Devon Ave., #512
Chicago, IL 60660
Phone: 800-318-6312
Web site: www.flyball.org

Orthopedic Foundation
for Animals (OFA)
2300 East Nifong Blvd.
Columbia, MO 65201
Phone: 573-442-0418
Fax: 573-875-5073
Web site: www.offa.org

Pet Industry Joint Advisory Council
1220 19th St., NW, Suite 400
Washington, DC 20036
Phone: 202-452-1525
Fax: 202-293-4377
E-mail: info@pijac.org
Web site: www.pijac.org

Pet Loss Support Hotline
College of Veterinary Medicine
Cornell University
Ithaca, NY 14853-6401
Phone: 607-253-3932
Web site: www.vet.cornell.edu/
public/petloss

Pet Sitters International (PSI)
201 East King St.
King, NC 27021-9161
Phone: 336-983-9222
Fax: 336-983-9222
E-mail: info@petsit.com
Web site: www.petsit.com

Therapy Dogs International, Inc.
88 Bartley Rd.
Flanders, NJ 07836
Phone: 973-252-9800
Web site: www.tdi-dog.org

UK National Pet Register
74 North Albert St., Dept 2
Fleetwood, Lancasterhire, FY7 6BJ
United Kingdom
Web site: www.nationalpetregister.org

United States Dog Agility Association, Inc. (USDAA)
P.O. Box 850955
Richardson, TX 75085-0955
Phone: 972-487-2200
Fax: 972-272-4404
Web site: www.usdaa.com

Veterinary Medical Databases
1717 Philo Rd.
P.O. Box 3007
Urbana, IL 61803-3007
Phone: 217-693-4800
E-mail: cerf@vmdb.org
Web site: www.vmdb.org

World Canine Freestyle Organization (WCFO)
P.O. Box 350122
Brooklyn, NY 11235-2525
Phone: 718-332-8336
E-mail: wcfodogs@aol.com
Web site: www.worldcaninefreestyle.org

Further Reading

Eldredge, Debra. *Dog Owner's Veterinary Handbook*. New York: Howell Book House, 2007.

Ewing, Susan. *Bulldogs for Dummies*. Hoboken, N.J.: Wiley Publishing, 2006.

Fishman, Abe, and Wil DeVeer. *American Bulldog* (Comprehensive Owner's Guide). Allenhurst, N.J.: Kennel Club Books, LLC, 2005.

Gagne, Tammy. *Animal Planet Bulldogs*. Neptune City, N.J.: T.F.H. Publications, Inc., 2007.

Harris, Dr. David. *The Bully Breeds*. Mission Viejo, Calif.: Bowtie Press, 2008.

Maggitti, Phil. *Bulldogs* (Complete Pet Owner's Manual), 2nd ed. Hauppage, N.Y.: Barron's Educational Series, 2007.

Morgan, Diane, and Wayne Hunthausen, DVM. *The Bulldog* (Terra Nova Series). Neptune City, N.J.: T.F.H. Publications, Inc., 2005.

Owens, Paul, and Norma Eckroate. *The Dog Whisperer: A Compassionate, Nonviolent Approach to Dog Training*, 2nd ed. Avon, Mass.: Adams Media, 2007.

Palika, Liz. *The Ultimate Pet Food Guide: Everything You Need to Know About Feeding Your Dog or Cat*. Cambridge, Mass.: Da Capo Press, 2008.

St. John Cooper, H. *Bulldogs and Bulldog Breeding* (A Vintage Dog Books Breed Classic). Warwickshire, England: Vintage Dog Books, 2005.

Internet Resources

http://www.healthypet.com

The Web site of the American Animal Hospital Association, which accredits animal hospitals throughout the United States and Canada.

http://www.akc.org/breeds/bulldog/index.cfm

The Bulldog breed standard can be found at this American Kennel Club Web page. The AKC's Web site (ww.akc.org) includes links to a great deal of information related to dog ownership.

http://www.aspca.org/pet-care/poison-control/

This Poison Control Center Web page provided by the American Society for the Prevention of Cruelty to Animals (ASPCA) is the best resource for poison-related animal emergencies.

http://www.avma.org

The American Veterinary Medical Association Web site offers a wide range of information for dog owners.

http://www.thebca.org

Bulldog fanciers can check the Bulldog Club of America's Web site for the latest information about Bulldog behavior, care, health, and training.

Publisher's Note: The Web sites listed on these pages were active at the time of publication. The publisher is not responsible for Web sites that have changed their address or discontinued operation since the date of publication.

http://www.hsus.org

The official Web site of the Humane Society of the United States offers valuable information about pet adoption as well as general pet care tips.

http://www.thekennelclub.org/uk

The Web site of the Kennel Club of the United Kingdom offers information and advice on dog welfare, health, training, and breeding.

http://www.petfinder.com

This Web site can help you find adoptable English Bulldogs through shelters and rescue groups in your area.

http://www.vetmed.wsu.edu

The Washington State University College of Veterinary Medicine Web site covers a wide range of pet health topics.

http://www.westminsterkennelclub.org

This Web site includes breed information, showmanship videos, and details about the Westminster Dog Show.

Index

Numbers in **bold italics** refer to captions.

Contributors

A dog owner all her life, **ELAINE WALDORF GEWIRTZ** writes about human and canine behavior, care, health, and training. The author of books and articles, Elaine is a multiple recipient of the prestigious Maxwell Award from the Dog Writers' Association of America. Her writing has garnered the ASPCA Humane Issues Award and the Wiley/Ellsworth S. Howell Award.

Senior Consulting Editor **GARY KORSGAARD, DVM,** has had a long and distinguished career in veterinary medicine. After graduating from The Ohio State University's College of Veterinary Medicine in 1963, he spent two years as a captain in the Veterinary Corps of the U.S. Army. During that time he attended the Walter Reed Army Institute of Research and became Chief of the Veterinary Division for the Sixth Army Medical Laboratory at the Presidio, San Francisco.

In 1968 Dr. Korsgaard founded the Monte Vista Veterinary Hospital in Concord, California, where he practiced for 32 years as a small animal veterinarian. He is a past president of the Contra Costa Veterinary Association, and was one of the founding members of the Contra Costa Veterinary Emergency Clinic, serving as president and board member of that hospital for nearly 30 years.

Dr. Korsgaard retired in 2000. He enjoys golf, hiking, international travel, and spending time with his wife Susan and their three children and four grandchildren.